PRIMER OF PHILOSOPHY

WORKS BY THE SAME AUTHOR.

PRIMER OF PHILOSOPHY. Pages, vi, 242. Cloth, $1.00.

THE RELIGION OF SCIENCE. Pages, vi, 103. 50 cents.

HOMILIES OF SCIENCE. Pages, x, 317. Cloth, gilt top, $1.50.

THE IDEA OF GOD. Third edition. Pages, 31. Paper, 15 cents.

THE NATURE OF THE STATE. Pages, xii, 56. Paper, 15 cents.

THE GOSPEL OF BUDDHA. Fourth edition. Pages, xvi, 275. Cloth, gilt top, $1.00.

THE PHILOSOPHY OF THE TOOL. Pages, 24. Paper, illustrated cover, 10 cents.

THE ETHICAL PROBLEM. Three Lectures. Pages, xv, 90. Cloth, 50 cents; Paper, 25 cents.

TRUTH IN FICTION. Tales with a Moral. Bound in white and gold. Gilt edges. Pages, 111, $1.00.

GOETHE AND SCHILLER'S XENIONS. Selected and translated. Pages, 162. Bound in album form. Gilt edges, $1.00.

KARMA: A Story of Early Buddhism. Unique Japanese art edition. Crêpe paper, tied in silk. Quaintly illustrated, 75 cents.

FUNDAMENTAL PROBLEMS. The Method of Philosophy as a Systematic Arrangement of Knowledge. Second edition, enlarged and revised. Cloth, $1.50.

THE SOUL OF MAN. An Investigation of the Facts of Physiological and Experimental Psychology. With 152 illustrative cuts and diagrams. Pages, xvi, 458. Cloth, $3.00.

THE OPEN COURT PUBLISHING CO.

324 DEARBORN STREET, CHICAGO.

PRIMER OF PHILOSOPHY

BY

DR. PAUL CARUS

REVISED EDITION

CHICAGO
THE OPEN COURT PUBLISHING COMPANY
1896

Copyright, 1893,
BY
THE OPEN COURT PUBLISHING CO.
CHICAGO.

PREFACE.

LEST the title of this booklet be misunderstood, the author must state that he here means by "Primer" a presentation of the subject in the plainest and most lucid form in which he could put it.

"The Primer of Philosophy" is not expressly designed to give instruction to beginners in philosophy, but it is, nevertheless, eminently available for that purpose. The uninitiated student will not be bewildered or mystified, in perusing its pages, by high-sounding words or unintelligible phrases, but will, despite this lack of learned adornment, find in them the information he desires The subject is presented with great simplicity so that its leading idea can be gathered by a mere glance at its contents. The most essential technical terms are explained, and the high practical importance of philosophy is never lost sight of.

The point of view adopted in this, as in other publications of the author, is new to the extent that it cannot be classified among any of the various schools of recent thought. It represents, rather, a critical reconciliation of rival philosophies of the type of Kantian apriorism and John Stuart Mill's empiricism. The reconciliation reached disposes for good of a number of fundamental problems, and, particularly, of that old *crux philosophorum*, the question of the nature of reason, and will, thus, after a long unsettled period of embarrassments in which all progress has ceased, set the ship of philosophy afloat again.

PREFACE.

For the philosophy of these latter days is indeed like a ship run aground. Her helmsmen themselves have declared that further headway is impossible; that philosophical problems in their very nature are insolvable, and that there can be, therefore, but one true philosophy—the philosophy of agnosticism, which indolently acquiesces in the profession of a modest *ignorabimus*. It is but natural that under such circumstances the proud craft was abandoned by the most gallant of her crew. There was no work left for bold inquirers; there was no hope of accomplishing anything; the ship was fast, and her sailors were told to seek consolation in the idea that she had reached at last her haven, and that her present resting place, the belief in the Unknowable, was the stratified wisdom of all ages.

Philosophy in former ages boldly led the van of human progress, but it has now ceased to be considered of any practical importance. The public smile sarcastically at the perplexities of its hopeless condition, and the scientist has got into the habit of ignoring it entirely. And why should he not? Philosophy has become more of a hindrance than a help to him, blockading his way and spreading a mist before his eyes. Thus, to the detriment of true science, the sciences have gradually degenerated into mere specialties; with their philosophical background, the various branches of scientific inquiry have lost all intercoherence and deeper significance.

All this must change; and if the spirit in which this book is written, be true, it will change.

A new vista is opened before our eyes in which philosophy will become what it ought to be. Philosophy is no longer doomed to lie in the stagnant swamp where progress has become impossible, but strikes out boldly for new fields of noble work and practical usefulness.

THE AUTHOR.

TABLE OF CONTENTS.

INTRODUCTION.

The Principles of Philosophy: Positivism, Monism, Meliorism 1

EXPERIENCE THE SOLE BASIS OF PHILOSOPHY.

Data 9
Objectivity and Subjectivity 12
Duality and Monism 16
Appearance Not Sham 21
Experience 26
Knowledge 37
Science 41
Truth 46

THE METHODS OF PHILOSOPHY DERIVED FROM EXPERIENCE.

Axioms 51
A Priori and A Posteriori 62
The Formal 78
The Problem of the Three Dimensions of Space 89
Reason 103
Abstraction 118
The Absolute 127
Noumena and Reality 133

THE PROBLEMS OF EXPERIENCE SOLVABLE BY THE METHODS OF PHILOSOPHY.

CAUSATION.

	PAGE
Cause and Effect	137
Cause and Reason	138
Reason and Consequence	140
A Distinction Needed	141
Aristotle on Causation	143
Confused Notions of Causation	145
Causation Not Mere Succession	152
Explanation and Comprehension	153
Causation as Transformation	155
Teleology	156
Free-Will	159
Fatalism and Necessitarianism	163
The Character of Nature	165

PSYCHOLOGY.

The Association Philosophy	173
Composites of Blended Memories	178
The Nature of Perceptions	179
Generalisation Prior to Cognition	181
Apperception and Consciousness	182
Apperception and Will	184
Ideas and the Life of Ideas	187
Psychological Terms	189

RELIGION.

Christianity	196
Idolatry	199
The Religion of Science	203

INTRODUCTION.

THE PRINCIPLES OF PHILOSOPHY: POSITIVISM, MONISM, MELIORISM.

THE philosophical principles which dominate modern thought can be expressed in the two names, POSITIVISM and MONISM, the one being complementary to the other. True positivism is monistic; true monism is positive.

POSITIVISM represents the principle that all knowledge, scientific, philosophical, and religious, is a description of facts. Natural laws are formulas describing facts with the greatest possible economy, that is, in the most concise and exhaustive manner. Our abstract concepts do not represent any absolute or metaphysical entities, they represent certain features, qualities, or relations of existence. They are not forces behind nature. There is not something beyond that mysteriously produces natural processes. The natural processes themselves are reality.

The facts of experience are specie, and our abstract thoughts are bills which serve to economise the exchange of thought. If the values of our abstractions are not ultimately founded upon the reality of positive facts, they are like checks or drafts for the payment of which there is no money in the bank.

This positivism is in several respects different from the French positivism of the Comtian school; and therefore we call it "the new positivism." Comte's and Littré's positivism is really an agnosticism. Instead of solving the basic problems of philosophy, Comte and his school declared them to be insolvable.

We may add that all thinkers imbued with the spirit of modern thought will agree to the maxim that science has to take its stand upon facts, although a Roman Catholic philosopher may consider some things as facts which a scientist of heretic England does not.

We regard it as a matter of principle that a world-conception cannot be based upon facts of a doubtful character, or upon historical facts such as have happened once and do not happen again. A world-conception can be based upon such facts only as can be proved to be correctly observed, admitting of a constant revision by experiment.

Natural laws, theories, or interpretations of facts, not only have to be based upon well-ascertained experience, but must also not stand in contradiction to facts of any kind. Any conception of facts which makes one fact appear to be contradictorily different from any other fact is suspicious and must be rejected,

INTRODUCTION.

for indeed the ultimate criterion of truth is consistency with those facts that are well established.

This implies the second principle of philosophical method, which may be called, in one word, MONISM.

* * *

MONISM is a unitary conception of the world. The world must be conceived as one inseparable and indivisible entirety.

Monism stands upon the principle that all the different truths are but so many different aspects of one and the same truth. Two truths may be complementary to each other, but there cannot be two truths contradictory to each other. There is but one truth, and that one truth is eternal.

Monism, in a word, signifies consistency. Those who oppose Monism do not know what they are contending against. If they knew, they would give up their contention; for who could propose so absurd a theory as to establish inconsistency as a philosophical principle?

The term MONISM is often used in the sense of "one-substance" theory, that either mind alone, or matter alone, exists. These views, generally called "materialism," and "idealism" or "spiritualism," are pseudo-monisms, and would better be called "henism"; * for either view attempts to explain the world from one

---

* The word "henism" is derived from εἷς, ἑνός, denoting the singular number. "Monism" is derived from μόνος, meaning alone or one in the sense of unique.

single concept, deriving therefrom all natural phenomena. Monism does not attempt to subsume all phenomena under one category, but remains conscious of the truth that spirit and matter, soul and body, God and world, are different. Yet, although they may be different, they are not separate entities, but abstract ideas, denoting certain features of reality.

Monism is not a finished system, but a reliable plan for a system. It admits of a constantly increasing realisation and of a further perfection. Its aim is a methodical arrangement of experience so as to present a unitary or consistent conception of the world.

The monistic idea of a unitary conception of the world has been constantly corroborated by the progress of science. We are far from maintaining that all problems have been solved, but we declare that whenever science has made an indubitable progress it consisted in some further realisation of monism in this or that field, and we cannot even conceive of any future progress of science or philosophy that could be of a different nature.

Whenever a scientific discovery seems to point toward a dualistic world-conception, it must be regarded as an unsolved problem until the dualism is overcome.

* * *

MONISTIC POSITIVISM, or POSITIVE MONISM is not a newfangled philosophy. It is, and has always been, the principle of all sound science. The positive and monistic maxims of philosophy were perhaps not sufficiently appreciated in former ages, but they are growing to be clearly understood now, and will in time lead to the abandonment of all transcendental, metaphysical, supernatural, and agnostic speculations. Positive monism will change philosophy into a systematisation of positive knowledge, which will be useful to the scientist because it serves him as a background to his special field of inquiry, explaining to him the methods of cognition. It will be useful to the moralist, because it affords him the most solid foundation of his ethics ; and to the preacher, because it will explain the evolution as well as the practical purpose of religion. It will help him to distinguish between the essential and unessential, the permanent and the transient, and thus enable him to reconcile his religion with science.

* * *

The truth of scientific discoveries is tested by experiments, and in the same way the truth of a philosophy is verified in its ethics. The best argument in favor of a philosophy is this, that people can live according to the maxims derived therefrom.

We call the ethics which we derive from the philosophy of systematised facts, MELIORISM.

By MELIORISM we do not understand a modified optimism. The word Meliorism is often used in the sense that, though the world is full of evil and misery at present, it will in time become good and perfect ;

that evolution tends to a constant amelioration which by and by will lead to the abolition of all pain and a condition of undisturbed happiness.

The meliorism here proposed does not share in the fond illusion of these dreams. We grant, indeed we claim that there is progress; we recognise, too, that much pain is lessened and the enjoyments of man are increased as well as refined. Yet we recognise at the same time that this progress is accompanied with an increased sensibility to pain, so that the average happiness is not increased even by the greatest advances of civilisation.

MELIORISM gives up for good the idea that a perfect, painless, and undisturbed happiness is attainable. Meliorism does not seek the value of life in pleasures and pleasurable feelings, but in the work performed. Life is a struggle, and that which makes life worth living is the moral aim which we pursue. Life has no value in itself; life is an opportunity for creating values. Life gains in value the more we fill it with worthy actions.

OPTIMISM believes that the world is good, or at least that the good outweighs the evil; PESSIMISM believes that the world is bad, and that life is not worth living because the evils of life are ineradicable. MELIORISM regards the world as neither absolutely good nor absolutely evil, yet it recognises that life has purpose; the very existence of evil imposes duties upon man, and the possibility of building up the good implies the ideal of moral aspirations. A careful consideration of the facts of experience teaches us to seek satisfaction not in the transient pleasures of enjoyments, which, as such, are empty and shallow, but in attending to the duties of life, the demands of which are comprised in the one word "morality."

EXPERIENCE THE SOLE BASIS OF PHILOSOPHY.

DATA.

BY "data" we understand given facts; they are the material out of which we construct our ideas, notions, and conceptions.

What are our data? What is their nature, and how have we to deal with them?

* * *

Kant uses frequently the word *Anschauung*,* which means atsight, understanding thereby the living presence of our perceptions. He has not, however, given any further explanation of the meaning of the term.

---

* The German word *Anschauung* is a translation of the Latin *intuitio*, yet the English word "intuition" has been used already for that mystical kind of cognition, which is supposed to take possession of a truth by a direct apprehension, as a prophet sees in his mind something that is not present.

Anschauung denotes the state of looking at a thing. It means originally, the sensation of sight, yet its usage is extended to comprise any other kind of sensation which apprehends an object directly by feeling its presence.

The German word *Anschauung* affords to the German mind the advantage of being vernacular. Its meaning is to be taken as the word implies it, and not in any figurative sense. The author has ventured to translate the German *Anschauung* by the Saxon "at-sight," which is a neology, but seems to him to express precisely what *Anschauung* means.

For further particulars see *The Monist*, Vol. II, No. 4, p. 527.

He has neither analysed it, nor did he call special attention to its paramount importance.

The living presence of our perceptions, our at-sights, that which we perceive directly, by sensation, our meaning-endowed feelings, are the data or given facts of experience; and the data of experience form the capital with which we operate. The philosopher, the scientist, the inventor, the preacher, the moralist, the practical man of life, all these have nothing in their mental possession except the data of experience, and maxims, notions, or theories, more or less hypothetical, more or less true, more or less erroneous, derived from them.

What are these data of experience that form, as it were, the pedestal upon which all knowledge rests.

These data of experience are many different kinds of states of consciousness, and we can distinguish in all of them three elements:

(1) The feeling.

That feature which all states of consciousness have in common is the element of awareness, which constitutes that something by which sense-impressions are felt. It is existence as existence is in itself. It is being as being is conscious of itself in immediate self-apperception. Awareness is, as it were, the stuff of which consciousness consists; it is the substance of the data of experience.

(2) The forms of feeling.

We distinguish in the data of experience those

features which are peculiar to the various states of consciousness constituting their differences in kind. There are sensations of sight, of hearing, of taste, of smell, of temperature, and of touch or resistance; and again every single sensation of the various senses is of a peculiar kind, which is due to a different arrangement or combination of the elements that compose a given sense-impression. We call them the forms of the different states of awareness.

(3) The meaning of feelings.

Not the least important quality of the data of experience is the meaning which they possess. A sensation of a certain kind leaves a certain trace, and this trace constitutes a disposition to be remembered. When the same kind of sensation is repeated, the memory of the former sensation is reawakened. The new sensation fuses with the memory of the old one, and by this fusion the new one is felt to be the same or similar. Thus sensations come to denote the conditions under which they originate; they signify the presence of certain somethings that are faced, of objects standing opposite, so as to be represented, or, as it were, mirrored, in feelings. These meanings of the data of experience are called "the contents" of the states of our consciousness.

The contents of the states of our consciousness are representations, and that which is represented in representations is called the object. The whole range of the objective world comprises all the things which we are wont to call reality.

The term "reality" is used in two senses. It means, first, everything that exists; and in this sense my states of consciousness are real. It means, secondly, thingishness or objectivity, and in this sense my states of consciousness are not real. Real, in this narrower sense of the word, is contrasted to ideal, and denotes only the contents of our data of experience, or that which is represented in our representations.

We use the term "reality," as a rule, in its broader sense; in its narrower sense it is, for the sake of clearness, better called "objectivity," or the thingishness of existence; and the thingishness or objectivity of existence shows throughout the same feature, which makes it appear as *matter moving in space*.

By objectivity we understand that which the data of experience, our atsights, mean or represent; by subjectivity we understand that which constitutes the feeling in which objects are represented.

OBJECTIVITY AND SUBJECTIVITY.

The terms "subjective" and "objective" have undergone a very curious transformation, for each of the two words denoted in mediæval times exactly its opposite.

Duns Scotus was the first to call attention to the contrast of subjective and objective; yet he called

EXPERIENCE.

"subjectum" that which underlies our thought as its subject-matter—a usage which is still observed in logic, grammar, and common parlance. The subject is the thing under consideration, and we still speak of the subject in a sentence, of the subject of a lecture, etc. Subjective, accordingly, was to Duns Scotus that which is the essential nature of the subject in this sense, viz., that which characterises the thing; it means thingish, or, as we now say, "objective."

Duns Scotus coined the term "objective" to denote that which does not belong to the thing or subject of thought. The term "objective" characterises to him the nature of thinking beings, that which pertains to ideas in which reality is represented. It is that which stands opposite the thing, which faces the subject under observation; it is the observer. Accordingly, in Scotus's terminology it means precisely that which we now call "subjective."

Descartes still employs the term "objective" in the sense of Duns Scotus, and the word "subject" is, at least in France and England, used to this day in common parlance in its old significance.

In the seventeenth century the term "subject" began to be used to denote the reality of the soul, and as soon as this usage was established so that Leibnitz could speak of the *subjectum ou l'âme même*, philosophers naturally understood by "subject" the thinking being, and by "subjective" that which characterises the thinking being.

Soon after Leibnitz, in the eighteenth century, the term "object" was used by German philosophers in contrast to *subjectum* or the thinking being in the sense of the German *Gegenstand* (a word coined to translate "object"), to denote that which is objected to us, which stands opposite us, which is the reality contemplated and reasoned about; and the German terminology has gradually been adopted by the other nations.

We now use the terms as the Germans fixed their meaning. Object is a synonym of thing or *Gegenstand*, and objective denotes the reality or thingishness of existence as we perceive it with our senses, while subjective is that which denotes the character of the thinking being, that which pertains to the representation of things, that which conceives them and reasons about them.

* * *

Objects and the whole world of objective existence appear to the thinking subject as matter moving in space. Objects are that which the meanings of our sensations, of our *Anschauungen*, of our atsights, purport to be. Objects, accordingly, are not full and whole realities, but abstracts of reality only. The whole reality contains both subject and object. On the other hand, purely subjective states and the whole realm of subjectivity are abstracts also. We can separate the subject from the object only mentally, not actually. In actual reality they are inseparable.

EXPERIENCE.

There is no subjectivity which is nothing but subjectivity, nor is there any objectivity which is nothing but objectivity. Objectivity in its nature as objectivity which appears to be matter moving in space, must face some other existence so as to be objective, so as to appear as matter moving in space. It must be perceived or at least it must affect something by impact, i. e., in a way which can be conceived as mechanical action.

Suppose that existence did not affect other existence. In that case it could not be said to exist; it would not be real. The peculiarity of existence consists in affecting other existences, and this constitutes its objectivity. "Matter moving in space" is a term by which we comprehend in a general way our means of representing the objectivity of existence.

*   *   *

The question has been asked, What are objects in themselves? Objects appear to be matter moving in space; they are represented in the feelings of a thinking subject as material bodies; but what are they in themselves? What is the nature of their own being?

The answer to this question is suggested by the facts of our own existence. The thinking subject appears to other thinking subjects as an object in the objective world. We are feelings, but we appear to other subjects as material bodies moving about in space.

No one has ever seen a feeling, no one has ever found among the objects of the objective world a pleasure, or a pain, or a sensation of any kind. We can only see motions, we hear sounds which are air-vibrations, we observe gestures which being such as we make when we feel pains, or pleasures, or sensations of a certain kind, we infer that the bodies before us have analogous sentiments. Thus we conclude that that which is a feeling in itself appears as a motion to other feeling beings, and *vice versa*, that which appears to us as a motion is in itself either a feeling or something analogous to feeling.

In other words: Our subjective existence appears objective to other subjects, and all objective existence is in itself subjective.

DUALITY AND MONISM.

While we say that every peculiar form of objectivity must be thought to be ensouled with an analogous subjectivity, we do not share the fantastic notions of the savage who believes that a rock, or a spring, or a planet possesses a soul and can be regarded as a sentient, or even a thinking being.

Feelings are the ultimate units of our conscious soul-life, but they need not for that reason be the ultimate atoms or elements of subjective existence. Feelings are most likely very complex processes; and the elements of which a thing consists need not be a miniature of the thing. The parts of a clock are not diminutive clocks. Thus the elements of feeling need as little be actual feelings as the properly human, the characteristic features of man, can be found in the single cells of which a human being consists.

Accordingly we say : Subjectivity is that something of existence from which under special conditions feelings originate ; and subjectivity is supposed to be a universal feature of existence.

It is difficult for us to imagine what the subjectivity of the gravitating stone or of the flame amounts to ; yet we do know that in inorganic nature there must be something analogous to our feelings on a lower scale. There is a subjectivity of an elementary kind.

The subjectivity of a flame is not soul as is our subjectivity, for the flame's motions are determined not by ideas or anything like ideas, but by what we call its physical and chemical qualities. The subjectivity of the flame is not endowed with meaning, while our soul consists of, and our actions are determined by, representations.

* * *

The duality of subjectivity and objectivity does not establish dualism, for subjectivity and objectivity are not two different things which in their combination form real existence. They are two abstracts made of one and the same thing.

Reality, or as the Germans call it, *Wirklichkeit* (i. e., effectiveness), is a sytem of interactions. Every fact is *work-like* or *wirklich*; it is a working, or a taking effect; it is a process of causation. As such it is a relation, and all relations have two, or rather three, aspects; they are triune.

Suppose we have two points A and B. If A affects B, we can represent their interrelation by $+AB$ or $-BA$. There is but one reality, the interaction between A and B. But we can express it in two ways, either from the standpoint of A or of B as $+AB$ or as $-BA$; the former is from the standpoint of A the subjective, the latter the objective aspect. But the interrelation that takes place between A and B is for that reason not a combination of $+AB$ and $-BA$.

Let AB be a feeling, or some subjective aspect of an event, and BA a motion, or the objective aspect of AB. We shall see at once that while AB is not BA, the interaction between A and B is but one reality and not a combination of two facts.

The thing A exists in itself as little as the thing B in itself, or the relation between A and B in itself. All three, A and B and the mere relation between A and B, are abstracts. When speaking of the one or the other of them we take a special aspect of things in which we neglect the other aspects.

Therefore, when explaining things and the nature of things, we have always to resort to other things. We can characterise the qualities of things only by de-

EXPERIENCE.

scribing their action in relation with other things. We can explain the nature of a chemical element only by stating how it will behave when brought into contact with other elements.

* * *

The eagerness of reaching a unitary conception too quickly has misled philosophers into two errors, which are known as the materialistic and the idealistic philosophies.

Materialism is that philosophy which regards the objectivity of the world as its true and exclusive reality; while, *vice versa*, idealism (or as we had better call it "spiritualism") is that philosophy which takes the subjectivity of the world as its true and exclusive reality. The former regards feeling, consciousness, and thought as a fleeting phenomenon that originated incidentally in the purely mechanical interaction of blind forces, while the latter regards the whole objectivity of the world as a fleeting phenomenon, as a mere sham, an illusion or dream of the thinking subject.

True monism does not forget that spirit and matter, soul and body, God and world are abstracts and not things in themselves. True monism is not reached by wiping out all distinctions, but by recognising their inseparable oneness.

The monistic view is equally opposed to idealism and spiritualism (i. e. subjectivism) on the one hand,

and to materialism or crude realism (i. e. objectivism) on the other hand.

The spiritual of man is not as the materialist imagines, a mere accidental by-play of the material action of his body. The feeling, the psychical, the mental, the spiritual, or by whatever names we may call the subjectivity of existence in its various phases, is the very heart of nature; it is existence as it is in and to and by itself. The materiality of existence and the mechanical display of nature's forces are the appearance only as which existence represents itself. Existence is spiritual all through and the evolution of mind is not a mere incident, a happy chance, but a necessary outcome of the very nature of being.

The idealist, on the other hand, proposes a wrong formulation of the problem when he asks: Does reality or the objectivity of our representations exist? We should ask, What do we mean by reality or objectivity? and by defining it as that which affects us somehow so as to produce by various impressions various kinds of feelings, we have a definite and clear conception of it, and to deny the reality of reality would be equivalent to denying the existence of existence, including our own being.

When we try to solve the problem whether or not reality is real, we trouble with a self-made puzzle. The genuine problem of idealism can only be to find a criterion between dream-sensations and reality-sensations. That kind of idealism which fails to see the difference may deny regularity in nature, but it cannot deny its reality; for even dreams and hallucinations are truly real. Dreams and hallucinations are sensations not less than other sensations. The feelings are actual and indubitable. The interpretation only which our straying mind puts upon them is wrong, so that further experiences will not justify the meaning attached to them.

APPEARANCE NOT SHAM.

Some idealists—we mainly refer to certain Hindu philosophers—have been fond of disparaging objective existence and the means by which we represent it. Matter moving in space being the appearance of existence, they have spoken of the sham, the illusion, the mockery of the senses. But is this contemptuous attitude justified?

Is the world of matter in motion, as reality represents itself to our senses, really an untrue picture of the world? Is sensation a lie? Most assuredly there is no truer or better representation of reality. The objectivity of nature is the only way in which it appears and, far from being a sham, a mockery, an illusion, or even a lie, it is a revelation.

The Hindu philosophers should, from their own premises think better than they do of the world of appearances, for it is the objectivity in which the subjectivity of nature presents itself.

The objective appearance of things is not only the only means but also an adequate and perfectly reliable means by which we can know what kind of reality we have before us. The objectivity of nature is the key to the world secrets.

Let us investigate the motions of matter, let us observe and study natural phenomenon, and we shall learn something of the souls of other creatures and things. This is a slow and a thorny way, but it is the only way, and it leads to truth.

Errors do not exist in the world of objective facts. Errors are children of the mind. There is neither good nor bad, neither right nor wrong, neither truth nor falsehood, except in mentality. Sensations are facts, not interpretations of facts: but the meanings attributed to sensations are of a mental nature. Sensations being given facts, there is no deception in them. They are the material out of which mind grows. The significance of sensations, however, the interpretation of facts, that which constitutes the mind of a feeling being, is subject to misconception.

There exists a bad habit of speaking of sense-illusion when wrong inferences from the sense-data are drawn. But the sense-data are quite correct, they do not lie, they do not deceive, the interpretation only is erroneous which is put upon the sense-data.

To represent sensations as sham is tantamount to denying the reality of facts.

The contempt of objective existence as a sham and the undue prominence which was given to subjectivity as if it were absolute reality and being in itself, led to a wrong ethics ; it led to world-flight and pessimism. The material world as it appears in sense-perceived appearances, it may be granted, is not and should not be called being as it is in itself, it is being as it appears to a sentient being. So we ourselves appear to other beings as material bodies, while in ourselves we are what is commonly called soul. While body is the soul as it appears, soul is the essence of the body as it is in itself. Soul and body, accordingly, are the two inseparable sides of our existence ; they are two abstracts made from one and the same reality, and the contempt of the one leading to a neglect of it will necessarily bring about a degradation of the other.

Monism, accordingly, instead of leading to the contempt of either body or soul, spirit or matter, should lead to their equal appreciation.

Here lies the one-sidedness of the Brahman-monism, and the fatal results to which it led are sufficiently known. The present state of India is the best evidence. There are undoubtedly some other causes that coöperated to bring about the downfall of the Hindu nations, but the weakness engendered by their pessimistic world-conception is certainly not the least among them, and we learn from India's fate how important are our basic religio-philosophical convictions. The once greatest nation, foremost among all peoples of the earth in learning, literature, science, wealth, war-like power, and religious enthusiasm, now lies in the most wretched state of helpless dependence. Their one-sided monism led to a dualism and taught asceticism as the highest virtue, and world-flight as the greatest ideal.

Taking this ground, we, on the one hand, cease to speak in terms of contempt about matter and motion, and the laws of motion. It is fashionable among certain philosophers of high standing* to regard the mechanical as something low and anti-spiritual; but their arguments do not carry conviction. On the other hand, we appreciate the importance of the soul, of thought, of consciousness. The soul is not a mere spectator superadded to the body and being without consequence. Our thoughts are not a redundant by-play of brain-motions, and consciousness is not an unnecessary and dispensable superfluity.

The laws of mechanics reveal to us, not the essence of spiritual existence, but, after all, certain modes of its activity. The essence of mind, which consists in the meaning that naturally develops out of feelings, is not mechanical; but without taking into consideration the modes of the mind's activity, we can never understand its moment and import.

* * *

The laws of mechanics, far from being anti-spiritual, are the means by which we learn to understand and

---

* Charles S. Peirce in his articles in *The Monist*.

objectively to represent the action of spiritual existence.

If the sense-wrought world of material existences is appearance, it is at the same time a revelation and should not be called a sham. If the essence of the body, its inner nature, its being in itself, is the soul, we can acquire knowledge of other souls through a knowledge of their bodily forms and of their actions only. Since our knowledge of self is insufficient, unless it be observed in its interaction with other existences, we cannot even know our own soul without drawing largely upon the resources of our objective experience.

Purely subjective experience teaches us only that we have feelings of a special kind; it teaches us the bare results and nothing about their causes. We feel something, say, for instance, a pain. Beyond this fact of a peculiar feeling we know nothing out of our own consciousness. That a certain pain is an ache to be located in a special tooth is a purely mental inference drawn from objective observation or experiment.

Subjectivity forms the condition, but objectivity furnishes the means and methods of experience. The development of mind is possible only by the interaction of reality, which to the acting and reacting being naturally appears an innerness and outerness.

Neither innerness nor outerness are the whole of reality. To know existence and to understand its nature, we must interpret the one with the assistance of the other.

We regard the objectivity of nature as the great apocalypse of existence. It is no sham, but a revelation; it is a disclosure of its being and a display of its reality.

EXPERIENCE.

Experience is the effect of events upon sentient beings.

The condition of experience is memory. Grant that in a world of changes sentient beings are possessed of memory and the result will be what is commonly understood by "experience."

That experience is the sole source of human knowledge has been doubted by three classes of men only: (1) by mystics, (2) by believers in supernaturalism, and (3) by Kant and strict Kantians.

Mystics believe that there exists some kind of inspiration which bestows at a glance and in full completeness knowledge which can otherwise be acquired only imperfectly and piecemeal by many years of experience. This extraordinary means of knowledge is called "intuition," because mystics describe their ecstacies as visions. We simply utter a tautology when we say that knowledge derived in a mystical way by intuition is "visionary" in the literal sense of the word; but the intuitionalist's "visionary" is now so discredited that the very word has become a synonym for the fantastic, the unreal, the fabulous, the chimerical, the impossible.

Believers in supernaturalism declare that some truths were not acquired in the natural way but by the special intervention of an extramundane God. They regard *revelation* as a better and more reliable source of knowledge than experience.

Of the truth which supernaturalists claim has been acquired by special revelation, two kinds may be distinguished: first, such moral truths as love of enemies and self-sacrifice for ideals higher than self, and secondly, mysterious statements concerning extramundane affairs. The former have been proved to be of natural growth; for they have been developed without any supernatural intervention among people who are entirely without the pale of the Israelitic, Christian, and Mohammedan religions.

The maturest and most careful investigations of ethical science show that all vices lead to destruction, and we have to regard the noblest and most elevated virtues as exactly those which, according to natural laws, possess the power of preservation. Moral truths, accordingly, are not unattainable, and if it were true that Jews, Christians, and Moslems did not and could not naturally develop their moral ideas, which in a less complete form were naturally developed among other nations, this would prove only the mental or moral inferiority of these races.

The second class of supernatural truths, i. e., mystical statements concerning extramundane affairs, are partly vague and partly absurd, so that they can neither be explained nor understood : they have simply to be believed. And this is the opinion of the supernaturalists themselves, stated in the sentence : *Credo quia absurdum.*

Kant is neither a mystic nor a supernaturalist ; yet he objects to the proposition that experience is the sole source of knowledge ; and Kant's objection is characteristic of his entire philosophy—indeed, it forms its starting-point.

Let us briefly review the antecedents of Kant's ideas.

Locke merely followed the old tradition of philosophical thought as handed down from Aristotle, as insisted upon by Bacon, as held by Spinoza, that experience is the sole source of knowledge. "Our observation," Locke said, "employed either about external sensible objects, or about the internal operations of our mind perceived and reflected on by ourselves, is that which supplies our understanding with *all* the materials of thinking." (Italics are ours.) "Essay on Human Understanding," II, ch. i.

Locke discards the theory of innate ideas proposed by Descartes and compares the mind to a *tabula rasa*, a white sheet of paper, on which all ideas are written through sense-experience. His theory is founded upon the principle of the peripatetical philosophy: *Nihil est in intellectu quod non antea fuerit in sensu.*

The weakness of Locke's system is apparent. If sense-impressions are comparable to the writing on a sheet of paper, whence is the mind that receives these sense-impressions ! It may be granted that nothing is *in* the intellect but that which has been before in the senses. This explains how the intellect can acquire knowledge by impressions, but it does not explain the intellect itself. Leibnitz accordingly extended the sentence into this form : *Nihil est in intellectu quod non antea fuerit in sensu,*—EXCIPE NISI IPSE INTELLECTUS. (Nothing is in the intellect which was not before in the senses—except the intellect itself.)

This weakness in Locke's system became apparent in his followers, especially in Hume. Hume granted that all ideas might be resolved into impressions except one, viz., that of necessary connection. We meet with "constant conjunctions" in experience, but not with necessity, and thus the basis of all science, the law of cause and effect, remains a mere assumption. This consideration made of Hume a sceptic.

Kant was aroused from his dogmatic slumber, as he states himself, by Hume's scepticism. But Kant saw what Hume had overlooked : that there are many more conjunctions to which we attribute necessity ; foremost among which are mathematical theorems, the certainty of which was never doubted, even by Hume.

Mathematical truths are not products of sense-impressions. Mathematical reasoning is purely formal. The sense-element is carefully eliminated from them.

And yet we have ideas of purely formal reasoning, and these ideas are not only perfectly clear, but have also been regarded since times immemorial as the model of all reliability. We do not hesitate to attribute to them universality and necessity.

Thus Kant concludes that there is another source of knowledge, which cannot be resolved into and which does not rise out of the experience of sense impressions. This other source is the pure understanding or pure reason.* Kant's "Critique of Pure Reason" was the result of this suggestion received from Hume.

* * *

We have now to call attention to the ambiguity with which the term "experience" is used.

Locke might have accepted our definition of experience, viz.: as the effect of events upon sentient beings; but the school to which he belonged regarded the sensational element of impressions, caused by these events, as sufficient to explain the rise of ideas. Hence the name Sensationalism. Hume and Kant followed Locke and the so-called school of sensationalism in the usage of the term "experience."

Kant understands by experience, as a rule, sense-experience. He defines it in his "Critique of Pure Reason" as "a cognition which determines an object by means of perception," meaning thereby the sensory element of sensations, for he contrasts experience with

---

* Kant fails to make a clear distinction between reason and understanding.

the formal cognition of mathematics, arithmetic, logic, and other sciences of pure reason.

But Kant is by no means consistent. On the contrary, he is very ambiguous in his usage of the word "experience"; and this is undoubtedly one main source of confusion, from which his dualistic conception of the *a priori* arises.

In one place Kant speaks of "experience as the product of our understanding after having worked out the raw materials of our sensations," while in another place he identifies it with sensuous impressions, saying that "empirical knowledge has its sources *a posteriori*, i. e. in experience," and distinguishing from this kind of experience the *a priori* or purely formal. Thus, experience is in one place the product of our mental activity and sensations, and in another only the sensuous impressions from which part of our knowledge comes, viz., the *a posteriori*. In the former sense the formal knowledge of the *a priori* has been worked into "experience"; in the latter sense "experience" is the sensory source of knowledge. In the former sense it is identical with knowledge; in the latter sense it is identical with sensation; and experience-in-the-latter-sense is one of the two sources of experience-in-the-former-sense.

Kant uses experience in a third sense, which comes nearest the popularly accepted meaning of the word. The third sense of the term slips in unawares, so that Kant does not feel a need of explaining it, as he incidentally does with experience in the sense of knowledge and of sensuous impressions. Experience in the third sense covers the meaning of the term as we use it; and we define experience as the (whole) effect of events upon sentient beings. This includes the sensory as well as formal elements of our sensations and also the conclusions which we draw from them.

Kant says that all knowledge begins with experience-in-the-third-sense (viz., sense-impressions of various forms to which we attribute various meanings). But it does not rise out of experience-in-the-second-sense (viz., sensuous impressions only), for he says experience-in-the-first-sense (viz., knowledge) is the product of our understanding and of experience-in-the-second-sense, i. e. sense-impressions.

The following words of Kant are the original of our paraphrase:

"That all our knowledge begins with experience there can be no doubt. For how is it possible that the faculty of cognition should be *awakened* into exercise otherwise than by means of objects which affect our senses and partly of themselves produce representations, partly rouse our powers into activity to compare, to connect, or to separate these, and so to convert the raw material of our sensuous impressions into a knowledge of objects which is called experience?" (Second edition.)*

We have italicised the word "awakened" because it is no mere figure of speech. According to Kant, the faculty of cognition exists, although in a latent state,

---

* See also the beginning of the Introduction to Kant's *Critique of Pure Reason*. The second edition deviates considerably from the first.

and has to be roused. It is its business to add something out of its *a priori* stock to the sensations offered *a posteriori*. The first edition is, perhaps, plainer in actually and unequivocally stating the preëxistence of our understanding:

"Experience is without doubt the first product which our understanding brings forth in working out the raw materials of sensations."

The *a priori* is supposed to exist in a latent form. It is roused by producing experience under the stimulus of sensations, the latter being experience in the second sense.

Sometimes it appears that experience in the second sense is most prevalent in Kant's philosophy, because he does not tire of telling us that the *a priori* does not arise out of experience; and then again he emphasises his definition of experience in the first sense.

When Professor Kiesewetter visited Kant (in 1788 –'89, and again in 1791) they discussed, every second day, between 11 and 12 A. M., philosophical topics, and Kant used to work out brief answers to questions proposed in the previous hours. In the first of these essays (the MSS. of which remained in the possession of Kiesewetter) Kant gives the following series of definitions:

"An empirical representation of which I am conscious is *perception*. That which I add in thought to the representation of the imagination, by dint of conception and comprehension (*compre hensio æsthetica*) of the manifold of perceptions, is the *empirical cognition of the object*, and the judgment which expresses an empirical cognition is *experience*."

This is experience in the first sense; it does not mean sense-impressions or sensations, but knowledge.

It is natural that this ambiguous usage of the term "experience" is a constant source of confusion, which proves very perplexing to the student of Kant's philosophy.

* * *

If by experience is to be understood the sense-element of experience only, it is quite natural that purely formal knowledge cannot be resolved into, or explained as arising from, experience. If, however, experience is "the judgment which we pass upon empirical cognition," we can derive formal knowledge from experience.

Experience, as we use the term, is not restricted to the sense-element alone. Sense-impressions possess certain shapes; they stand in relations among themselves; they are not merely sensory, but contain also a formal element. And this formal element of experience is not less, but rather more, important than the sense-element.

At a certain stage of the evolution of mind, a sentient being learns to think in such abstracts of purely formal ideas as numbers. Numbers are abstracts of pure form. They are derived from experience, i. e., not from the sensory features of experience, not from experience as Kant uses the term, but from the formal element of experience. By counting, we construct a system of numbers which soon becomes, as a schedule of reference, a most essential part of the mind.

When stating that my table has four legs, I do not derive the idea "four" by a direct abstraction from the entire sense-impression called "table," but by reference to that system of numbers in the mind which existed *a priori* to the present experience, i. e., long before I saw this table.

The same is true of other pure forms. As numbers have naturally arisen by viewing acts of counting abstractly, so all the other formal sciences are domains of wholesale abstraction. Mathematics starts with purely formal space-relations and constructs of them systems which, in the same way as numbers, serve as models and schedules of reference. Logic starts with purely formal thought-relations and constructs such frameworks of thought as the categories, which serve as mental shelves or pigeon-holes for an orderly and systematic arrangement of ideas.

According to Kant, sense-experience by itself is blind, and formal cognition by itself is empty; and indeed perfect knowledge would not be possible if experience consisted either of its sense-elements alone or of the formal alone. A perfect knowledge of realities becomes possible only by a coöperation of both. The formal and the sensory are the web and woof of knowledge.

Kant saw that the formal and the material (viz., the

sense-element of experience) are inseparable in the subjective realm of thought, but he did not see that they are also inseparable in the objective realm of real existence. He regarded the formal element of real things as added to the material by the mind, as if formless things could exist. Considering the fact that events can be explained only when conceived as transformations, the tracing of form being the method of cognition, we can no longer wonder that things become unknowable to Kant.

Kant is a very great philosopher; he is a giant among thinkers. Nevertheless, it is true that his great fame was not so much due to his greatness, as to his mistakes. He propounded a problem to mankind which has kept philosophical minds busy ever since. His ability consisted in seeing the problem, not in solving it. His own solution, or rather lack of solution, (for he never inquired into the origin of what he termed the *a priori*), cast a glamor of mysticism over his philosophy which had not been intended by him but proved a source of great fascination to all those minds who take delight in the chiaroscuro of a systematic, or apparently systematic, ignorance. And this class of thinkers—the philosophasters of mankind—are still in the majority. Their applause, like that of the galleries in the theatre, counts most.

After this exposition of the objections made to the doctrine that experience is the sole source of human knowledge, we need hardly add that modern science and philosophy are to be based upon experience.

No other source has as yet been proved reliable. That which Kant calls the *a priori* is a systematic construction of the formal elements of experience. The visionary knowledge of intuition has been entirely abandoned, and the theory of a supernatural revelation is an erroneous interpretation of the religious experiences of past ages. God reveals himself to mankind in exactly these data of experience; and religion will not be free from pagan elements until this truth is recognised.

KNOWLEDGE.

We define knowledge (1) as a representation of facts in sentient symbols; and (2) as a description of facts (Kirchhoff). In the former sense we limit the term to sentient beings, in the latter we apply it generally. The usage of the verb "to know" is limited exclusively to the former sense, for we do not say, for instance, that a book "knows" something. The latter sense is more general. We say that a man has knowledge, and also that a book contains knowledge.

The root of the words *to know, gnoscere*, γιγνώσ-κειν, *erkennen*, etc., is the same as in *ken, can, können*, denoting an ability to do something.* It signifies the

* The verb "to know" is used in Genesis iv, 1, in the sense of "causing to bring forth, or to produce." So the German *erkennen* (a reflex causative form of *kennen*, meaning "causing one's self to know") and the Greek γιγνώσκειν have the same double meaning. Is it a strange coincidence only or a fact of

mental disposition which makes a man fit to accomplish his purpose. It is his state of being acquainted with the facts with which he has to deal.

What is the nature of this state, and how does it originate?

The origin of knowledge, i. e., the act of becoming acquainted with things, of acquiring knowledge, of perceiving, is called cognition.

A sentient being is exposed to impressions of the surrounding world. The various objects make various impressions upon the different senses, and these impressions are remembered. Certain characteristic features of their forms remain and can be revived by an appropriate stimulus, so as to be felt again. As soon as a certain event (say a ray of sunshine previously registered by the eye as light and by the skin as a peculiar kind of warmth) impresses itself upon the sense-organs, it revives the memory-structures of the same kind. The feeling of the present sense-impression is felt to be the same in kind as those prior sense-impressions, the vestiges of which are preserved in the revived memory-structures. The reference of a sense impression to the memory-structure of its class is a primitive perception, and perception is the simplest act of cognition.

deeper significance that these verbs are used to express two so heterogeneous acts as "knowing and begetting"? If it is a confusion between two roots of a similar or the same sound, it is certainly very, very old and dates back to the period before the separation of the various Aryan branches. Should the coincidence arise from the same conception which in more recent times gave two meanings to the words "potent" and "impotent"?

EXPERIENCE.

Facts are pictured in sensations, and these pictures represent the facts. A certain feeling has come to stand for a certain object, event, or phenomenon. The presence of this feeling signifies the presence of its respective and analogous object, event, or phenomenon, and this state of representativeness of various feelings, in its higher perfection, is called knowledge. On a higher level of mentality facts are described in names or word-symbols,* and these names represent whole classes of facts.

Knowledge is rendered definite by naming. A sentient being can be said to really know a thing only when he has named it. We know only that which we can clearly describe in words. Names label things and enable us to handle them in our minds without difficulty. They are symbols of the essential features of things.

Briefly, knowledge is an appropriate representation of facts in mental symbols, and the purpose of knowledge is the ability to deal appropriately with facts.

The amount of mentality in a mental being is measured by its knowledge, or rather by its ability of operating with knowledge. Knowledge is that which constitutes the power of mental beings, and without knowledge man's dignity would be naught. Knowledge is and must be the basis of all action ; for actions without knowledge are mere reflex motions.

---

* Mathematical and algebraic symbols must in this connection also be regarded as words.

Knowledge being of paramount importance, the acquisition of knowledge forms an indispensable and the most prominent department in human life. The acquisition of knowledge is the sphere of science.

The aim of science is to make knowledge not only reliable, but also handy. The former is obtained by criticism, the latter by classification, and the two together are called "system."

System means the arrangement of all parts into one whole. A set of facts or events, in order to be systematic, must be formulated so as to include, in a methodical order, all possibilities. This will exhaust the subject and at the same time allow us to survey the whole field, as it were, at a glance. System renders facts *übersichtlich*.* Having knowledge systematically arranged, we can readily assign new facts of a well-known class to their proper places in the system; we understand them at once and can predetermine the course of the events of such a class even previous to observation. We can also exercise criticism. We can judge of the reliability of accounts concerning facts, for we recognise at once contradictory elements as inharmonious with the rest.

Thus, on the one hand, system implies the com-

---

* An appropriate word is missing in English to denote the German *übersichtlich* and *Uebersichtlichkeit*, "surveyable and surveyability." Surveyability is more than "clearness" or "perspicuity"; it is a systematic arrangement in which one readily finds one's bearings. It is that order which makes a domain of science easily surveyed. Surveyability is attained by methodical arrangement; it is the product of "system"; it is the advantage derived from methodical arrangement.

pleteness of parts presented with greatest economy, and, on the other hand, affords a means of criticism for the elimination of faulty statements, contradictions, and errors.

SCIENCE.

We propose the following five definitions of science: (1) Knowledge, i. e., a description of facts. (2) Truth, i. e., a correct description of facts. (3) The search for truth. (4) The methodical search for truth. (5) The methods of searching for truth.

The Latin *scientia*, from which the word "science" is derived, bears a similar etymological relation to *scire* (i. e., "to know") as the German *Wissenschaft* to *wissen* and the English noun *knowledge* to its verb *to know*.* It means, originally, the stock of knowledge we have, and knowledge is "a description of facts."

Knowledge, it must be understood, has to be a correct description of facts; it must be true. The facts must be well ascertained and unmistakably stated. Knowledge means, *eo ipso*, correct knowledge; and correct knowledge is called "truth."

Science, however, as the term is commonly used, is not only the stock of knowledge on hand, but also and especially our endeavor to acquire knowledge; it is "the search for truth."

---

* The ending "ledge" is a distorted form of M. E. *leche* or *lac*, which appears also in wedlock. Its root, like that of *lay*, a song, denotes sporting or playing. It is connected with Germ. *Leich*, a song of irregular construction, the root of which is found in Goth. *laikan*, to dance, and Anglo-S. *lâcan*, to frolic.

Science, as the search for truth, presupposes our desire for truth and includes the way to reach it. The methods of science demand : (1) The exact observation of phenomena ; (2) the tracing out of their determinative factors ; (3) a discriminative statement of the phenomena under observation in comprehensive formulas, called natural laws ; (4) a systematising of natural laws ; (5) if possible, tests by experiment, and (6) the applications of the results of science to practical life.

As the total amount of matter and energy remains constant in the whole universe, science, in order to trace the determining factors, has to deal with changes of form, which in their succession are called causes and effects.

Science, above all, widens the range of experience, by the discovery of new facts ; it further purifies our knowledge by the elimination of contradictions and errors ; it also systematises the description of facts, so as to survey them with the greatest economy possible ; moreover, it aims at completeness, so as to exhaust the subject and comprehend in its formulas all possible cases ; finally, it makes its statements serviceable to practical ends.

It is the methods of searching which make the search for truth truly scientific, and when we wish to emphasise this, we define science as "the methodical search for truth."

The methods of science have come to be called

"science" themselves, because of their importance in the search for truth, as forming the essential characteristic of that which is to be regarded as scientific. In this sense we say: Science is "the methods of searching for the truth"; and these methods consist, as Mach has observed, in an "economy of thought."

The purpose of science is and remains truth, i. e., correct knowledge, or an accurate and exhaustive statement of facts. And the purpose of truth is its application to practical life in the various fields of industry, of art, and of moral conduct.

* * *

The basis of science is experience. Experience being the effect of events upon sentient beings, is a psychical phenomenon, and thus it is obvious that all science has a psychical basis. This, however, does not imply the conclusion that all sciences are merely branches of psychology.

Every single science investigates a special province of facts, and the limits of this province are artificially established by abstraction. Chemistry investigates the chemical qualities of things, physics the physical, and psychology the psychical. Botany collects and systematises all knowledge concerning plant-life, zoölogy does the same for animal life, and so on. But there is nothing in the world which consists of chemical qualities alone. The chemist confines his attention only to the chemical qualities of his objects of investigation, and leaves out of sight their psychical or any other properties. The domains of the different sciences overlap one another, and their barriers are erected simply for the sake of order and arrangement. We have to build up our knowledge piecemeal by limiting our attention now to this and now to that fact, and the limitation of each special science is a wholesale act of abstraction.

Thus psychology, although psychic facts are the basis of all experience, has quite a special province of its own. Psychology is the science which deals with the functions of the soul, i. e., it investigates the province of meaning-freighted feelings. The domain, for instance, of the physicist is limited to the physical qualities of things; so he excludes all the rest and accordingly also neglects the fact that all our physical knowledge is possible only because we are sentient beings. He takes for granted the whole state of things which make physics as a science possible and leaves their investigation to other men, or, if he desires to undertake it himself, defers it to another occasion. If this were not so, a general confusion would prevail and we might consider any science as a part of any other science. We might regard astronomy as a branch of logic, because the astronomer has to think in words (mathematical symbols being here included under the term "word"), or, *vice versa*, logic as a branch of astronomy, because the logician exists only as an inhabitant of one of the celestial bodies.

The world being thus divided among the sciences, must not philosophy, like the poet in Schiller's poem, "*Die Theilung der Erde*," leave the throne of Zeus empty-handed? There is seemingly nothing left; indeed, according to the Comtian idea of positivism, philosophy is nothing but a hierarchy of the sciences. Comte, in order to elaborate a positive philosophy, thought it necessary to present in a very voluminous work abstracts of the various sciences. This was a mistake, for, first, abstracts of the various sciences are better made by specialists, and, secondly, philosophy has other duties than that of dabbling in the spheres of the different sciences.

What, then, is the domain of philosophy?

Although all the different sciences have taken away their parts, there are left some very important objects for investigation: (1) The relations among the sciences, which make of them a systematic whole, so that their unity is conceived as a consistent world-conception; (2) the basis of all the sciences, and the scientific method, including the tools of scientific inquiry, which are such ideas as cause and effect, natural law, knowledge and cognition, experience, reason, truth, the criterion of truth, etc.; and (3) the practical application of the sciences as a world-conception to our own existence, with a view to gaining an insight into the nature of being, and the duties which it imposes.

An investigation of these subjects is of great importance and constitutes an abstract domain of its own.

Yet, as all the sciences are inseparable from each other, so philosophy is inseparable from the sciences. Its field is not outside them, but within them. A philosopher must also be a scientist; he must be imbued with the spirit of exact scientific inquiry, as, *vice versa*, the scientist must be a philosopher; he must understand the relation of his specialty not only to the other specialties, but also to the whole system of their common philosophical world-conception.

TRUTH.

Truth is correct knowledge, i. e., a statement of facts that is perfectly reliable. In other words: Truth is the agreement of a representation with the object represented.

No objection can be made to Thomas Aquinas when he defines truth as "*adæquatio intellectus et rei*," which, in more modern form, means "conformity of thought to thing." *Intellectus*, or thought, is the mental symbol, the idea, the conception of something, and *res* is the reality represented in the mental symbol of an idea, it is the object thought of.

Truth, accordingly, is the adequateness of a relation, to wit, of a mental relation. Without mind no truth. Truth does not dwell in non-mental facts. It is a misnomer to speak of objects or objective facts as being true. Facts are real, while the facts represented, i. e., statements of fact, if correct, are true.

A single sense-impression is a fact, but the perception of a sense-impression as a certain object is either true or untrue. Facts are real, or, if they do not exist, unreal; ideas are true or untrue.

There is a great difference between truth and reality. The facts of reality are always single, concrete, and individual. Every fact is a *hic* and *nunc*. It is in a special place, and it is as it is at a certain time. All facts are definite and of a particular kind. Yet truth, although representing facts, i. e., objects, or relations among objects, is never a concrete object, nor is it a *hic* or a *nunc*. It rises above facts, and views facts from a higher standpoint.

The simplest truths are statements as to the reality of facts; they are declarations that a certain thing, or event, or relation, does or did or will, does not or did not or will not, obtain. Higher truths are the statements of natural laws, describing certain regularities of facts in general formulas. Truth accompanies mind in its growth; and the higher a mind rises, of the more consequence will be the truth or untruth of its ideas.

The kinship of truth with mind endows truth with a generality that is lacking in the particularity of the single facts.

We cannot speak of the truth of mere sensations. The sense-organs furnish us with facts; they present certain data; and if our sense-organs perform their work with sufficient regularity, they furnish under the same conditions the same sensations. Properly speaking, we cannot say that there is truth in these sensations; they are as yet non-mental realities. Yet, when sensations are recognised as representing certain objects, i. e., when they become perceptions, they acquire the power of being either true or untrue. Perceptions are elementary judgments; they are the first mental functions, and from them the mind rises into existence. Should it happen that a sensation is registered in a wrong place, it will be mistaken; it will cause errors. Thus truth originates together with mind. Truth and error are the privilege of mind.

The development of mind means the development of truth. Sentient beings observe in a certain group of facts, in spite of all variety, some features of sameness. Such features are noted by brutes, then named by man, and, finally, in the scientific phase, they are expressed in exact formulas. These formulas are called natural laws. If a natural law describes all the cases precisely and exhaustively, we call it a truth.

Truth in one sense is objective; it represents objects or their relations conceived in their objectivity. in their independence of the subject. This means that the representation of certain objective states will, under like conditions, agree with the experience of all subjects—i. e., of all feeling beings having the same channels of information.

Truth, in another sense, is subjective. Truth exists in thinking subjects only. Truth affirms that certain subjective representations of the objective world can be relied upon, that they are deduced from facts and agree with facts. Based upon past experience, they can be used as guides for future experience. If there were no subjective beings, no feeling and comprehending minds, there would be no truth. Facts in themselves, whether they are or are not represented in the mind of a feeling and thinking subject, are real, yet representations alone, supposing they agree with facts, are true.

We have distinguished between true and real. We have further to distinguish between true and correct. Purely formal statements, such as $5 \times 5 = 25$, have no direct, but only indirect reference to objects. They are empty forms which have to be filled with contents from the realm of our experience. General usage agrees in denominating such statements of purely formal construction, if made with strict consistency, according to the rules of our mental operations, not as "true," but as correct.

The very name of truth has something holy about it. And rightly so! For if the All-existence in which we live and move and have our being is God, truth, viz., the representation of this All-existence, is God's revelation. Christian mythology calls God our father, and the word of truth, or the Logos, his only begotten son. It is the mission of Christianity to found an empire of truth, the kingdom of heaven upon earth, and this empire of truth which is within us (i. e., in the souls of men) must be acquired by our own efforts, or, to use the words of Christ, "The kingdom of heaven suffers violence," whenever men are eagerly searching for the truth.*

Considering the relation between mind and truth, it is natural that *mind yearns for truth*. The yearning for truth constitutes the deepest impulse of the mind. It cannot be otherwise, for *truth is the fulfilment of mind*. Truth, however, is a correct representation of facts not only as they are now and here, but also as, according to the conditions which constitute a given state of things, they must be here and everywhere. Mind expands in the measure that it contains and reflects the eternity and universality of truth.

The criterion of truth is the perfect agreement of all facts, of all interpretations and explanations of facts, among themselves. If two facts, such as we conceive them, do not agree with each other, we must revise them ; and it may be stated, as a matter of experience, that our mind will find no peace until a monistic conception is reached. A monistic conception is the perfect agreement of all facts in a methodical system, so that the same law is recognised to prevail in all instances, and the most different events are conceived as acting under different conditions, yet in accordance with the same law.

---

* We read in Matthew ii, 12: "And from the days of John the Baptist until now the kingdom of heaven suffereth violence, and the violent take it by force," which means that it is obtained only by strenuous effort.

THE METHODS OF PHILOSOPHY DERIVED FROM EXPERIENCE.

AXIOMS.

SUPERSTITIONS are much more common than is generally assumed, for they not only haunt the minds of the uneducated and uncivilised, but also those of the learned. Science is full of superstitions, and one of the most wide-spread of its superstitions is the belief in axioms.

"Axiom" is defined as "a self-evident truth."

It is not the peasantry who believe in axioms, but some of the most learned of the learned, the mathematicians; and since mathematics, with all its branches, is a model science, the solid structure of which has always been admired and envied by the representatives of other sciences, so that they regarded it as their highest ambition to obtain for the results of their own investigations a certainty equal to the certainty of mathematical arguments; not much offense was taken by any one at the notion that all the sciences might start with axioms, and that there are some simple and self-evident truths, which need not and cannot be proved.

Euclid does not use the term "axiom." Euclid begins his geometry with "definitions" (ὅροι), "postulates" (αἰτήματα), and "common notions" (κοιναί ἔννοιαί). Aristotle, however, repeatedly uses the term and defines it in his Analytics once as "the common principles from which all demonstration takes place" (I, 10, 4), and in another passage as "that immediate principle of syllogistic reasoning, which a learner must bring with him" (I, 2, 6).

Some of Euclid's postulates, and his common notions, were collectively called axioms by his followers; the latter are "axioms" 1-9, the former 10-12. The most important of the common notions is, "Things which are equal to the same thing are equal to one another"; the most important of the postulates, "Two straight lines cannot enclose a space."

That Newton called the laws of motion "axioms," need not be mentioned here. His usage of the word is simply a misnomer.

* * *

It is a strange idea that there can be truths which need no proof, but millenniums have passed without its being scarcely doubted. If the fundamental truths of mathematics, with the assistance of which all the theorems are to be proved, must be taken for granted, does not the whole of mathematics remain unproved? And if mathematics be permitted to start with axioms which must be taken for granted, why should not philosophy and religion have their confessions of faith, too?

Schopenhauer, one of the most radical philosophers, does indeed take the view that the whole of mathematics remains unproved. He says:

"That that which Euclid demonstrates is correct, we must concede according to the principle of contradiction; but why it is so, we are not informed. Accordingly, we almost have that uncomfortable sensation which we experience after a trick of legerdemain, and, indeed, Euclidean proofs are remarkably similar to it. Almost always truth comes in through the back door. It is found *per accidens* from some incidental circumstance. Sometimes apagogic argument closes the doors, one after the other, and leaves open only one into which we enter for no other reason. Often, as in the Pythagorean theorem, lines are drawn, and we know not why. Afterwards we notice that they were snares, which unexpectedly close, and thus compel the assent of the student, who now has to accept what remains to him in its interconnection perfectly incomprehensible. Thus we can go over the whole Euclid without really acquiring a true insight into the laws of spatial relations, or, instead of them, learn by heart only some of their results. This kind of cognition, which is rather empirical and unscientific, is comparable to the knowledge of a physician, who is acquainted with diseases and cures without knowing their connection.

"Euclid's logical method of treating mathematics is unnecessary trouble and crutches for healthy legs. . . . The proof of the Pythagorean theorem is stilted and insidious." (Schopenhauer, "Welt als Wille und Vorstellung," Vol. I, p. 83.)

Schopenhauer's view is not without foundation. Grassmann, one of our greatest mathematicians and the pathfinder of new roads in his science, says, concerning mathematical arguments:

"Demonstrations are frequently met with, where, unless the theorems were stated above them, one could never originally know what they were going to lead to; here, after one has followed every step, blindly and at haphazard, and ere one is aware of it, he at last suddenly arrives at the truth to be proved. A demonstration of this sort, leaves, perhaps, nothing more to be desired in point of rigidity. But scientific it certainly is not. *Uebersichtlichkeit*, the power of survey, is lacking. A person, therefore, that goes through such a demonstration, does not attain to an untrammelled cognisance of the truth, but he remains—unless he afterwards, himself, acquires that survey—in entire dependence upon the particular method by which the truth was reached. And this feeling of constraint, which is at any rate present during the act of reception, is very oppressive for him who is wont to think independently and unimpededly, and who is accustomed to make his own by active self-effort all that he receives." (Grassmann, "Die lineale Ausdehnungslehre, ein neuer Zweig der Mathematik," Introduction, page xxxi.)

Schopenhauer's criticism is good, but his method of mending the fault is not satisfactory. He makes of the whole structure of mathematics one great axiom and proposes to treat all mathematical truths in the same way as axioms. He proposes to prove them directly by intuition, to let them appear as self-evident, and imagines that no further argument is needed.

Says Schopenhauer:

"In order to improve the methods of mathematics, it is above all necessary to give up the prejudice that proved truths have any superiority over those which are intuitively known, or the logical argument, resting upon the principle of contradiction, over the metaphysical, which is immediately evident; and the pure intuition of space belongs to the latter class.

"That which is most certain and always incomprehensible is the contents of the principle of sufficient reason." (l. c., Vol. I, pp. 87-88.)

Grassmann pursues the opposite method. While Schopenhauer makes all mathematical theorems axiomatic, thus introducing into it a peculiar mysticism; Grassmann proposes to discard axioms altogether. He says:

"Geometry at the present day, still lacks a scientific beginning. The foundation on which the entire structure rests, suffers from a flaw that necessitates a complete reconstruction of the system. . . .

"The flaw, the presence of which I propose to show, is most easily recognisable in the concept of the plane. Taking the definition given in the systems of geometry, with which I am acquainted, I find it to be assumed fundamentally therein, that a straight line which has two points in common with a plane falls wholly within the plane;—be it that this is tacitly accepted (as Euclid has done), or embraced in the definition of a plane, or propounded, finally, as a distinct axiom. The first case,—where the assumption is tacitly made,—is on its face unscientific; while the second, as I shall presently show, can with no more reason pretend to the requisites of scientific character. . . .

"The only remaining course, therefore, in case we wished to hold to the method of geometry hitherto pursued, would be to convert that proposition into an axiom. But, if an axiom can be avoided, without having to introduce a new one in its stead, it must be done; even though it should bring about a complete reconstruction of the whole science. For, in this way, the science must gain substantially in simplicity. . . .

"The abstract methods of mathematical science know no axioms at all; the initial proof, in these methods, is brought about by the combination of predications; use being made of no other law of progression * than the universal one of logic that that which is predicated of a series of objects so as to apply to each separately, can be predicated in fact of each separate object belonging to that series. To set up as an axiom this law of progression, which, as we find, embraces merely an act of reflection upon what was intended to be said by the general proposition, can occur to no mathematician; this is done, improperly, in logic; and sometimes even it is attempted to be proved in that science."

Grassmann finds that "in geometry only those truths are left as axioms which are derived from the conception of space." Such truths, however, are not axioms in the proper sense of the term, but statements of fact which are true if verified by experience.

The methods of mathematical reasoning are rigidly formal thought-operations; they are, to use Kant's terminology, "absolutely *a priori*"; but the material which forms the substratum of mathematics consists only in part of products of rigidly formal thought-operations. Some notions concerning space which have been derived by experience slip in unawares, which, according to Grassmann's method, had better have been systematically formulated and propounded at the very beginning.

The notion of space upon which mathematics is based may briefly be formulated thus:

The constitution of space is throughout the same,

---

* What Grassmann calls the law of progression, is, as we should say, the consistency of mental operations, the nature of which, as we shall see in the articles, "The Formal" and "Reason" of this book, may be formulated as a sameness of operation producing a sameness of result.

being in all its places and directions three-dimensional, which means that three coördinates are needed to determine from any given point any other point.

This implies that equality is conceivable with difference of place and direction; so that the products of the same constructions in different places will be the same—a maxim formulated in Euclid's eighth axiom.

Geometry, now generally called Euclidean geometry, presupposes the existence of a plane. The nature of a plane is described in Euclid's eleventh and twelfth axioms as follows: "Two straight lines cannot enclose a [finite] space."

All the proofs by which it is attempted to demonstrate these axioms either presuppose what they are meant to prove or fail to prove it.

How can we escape the difficulty?

Suppose we construct with a pair of compasses a circle by keeping one point steady and allowing the other to describe a line which will return into itself. We might rack our brains in vain to find a logical proof for the statement that all the circle's radii will be equal, without assuming that all the points of the circumference remain at an equal distance from the centre. This latter, however, is the same as the former; and both are such as they are by construction.

The so-called Euclidean plane must be made such as it is by construction, and the possibility of constructing other planes is by no means excluded. How this construction is to be accomplished it is not for us to say. Euclid's eleventh and twelfth axioms simply serve to characterise the nature of the plane in which we proceed to construct our geometrical figures.

* * *

It is a matter of course that axioms, being out of place in mathematics, are out of place in any of the sciences and also in philosophy.

The bottom rock to which we have to dig down in all our investigations are not principles, or maxims, or axioms, but facts. Such things as principles and maxims have to be derived from facts, and axioms must be dispensed with altogether.

Obviously, Euclid's "common notions" are not axioms; but must we not regard his postulates as such?

Euclid's postulates are rules of reasoning specially adapted to mathematics, which, however, in a general form, are universally applicable in all logical reasoning.

Are not these rules of reasoning self-evident? Are they not principles which must be granted before we begin to agree, and must they not therefore be accepted as axioms?

The rules of reasoning have often received the name of axioms, but we cannot allow that their authority can be regarded as above investigation and proof.

The philosophical world has always vaguely felt that axioms are inadmissible in philosophy. The various philosophers have tried either to prove them or to do without them, to evade them.

At present it is generally supposed that we have to accept either the one or the other horn of this dilemma : either axioms are the result of an elaboration of particular experiences, i. e., are, like all other knowledge concerning the nature of things, *a posteriori*, or they are conditioned by the nature of human reason, they are *a priori*. The most prominent representative of the former view is John Stuart Mill; of the latter, Kant.

Kant replaces the name axioms in mathematics by the word "principles" of mathematics, but the fact remains the same ; he regards the mathematical principles as self-evident and directly apprehended by way of intuition. Being necessary and universally valid they are *a priori*. Indeed, to Kant, the whole field of the *a priori* is an empire of axiomatic truths, and Schopenhauer, his disciple, was more consistent than the master, as he accepted this consequence.

Mill discards not only axioms, but also the necessity and universal validity which should be the distinctive feature of axioms. To him axioms are generalisations of single experiences, but, being exceptionally simple and frequent, they possess, though not necessity, yet after all a quite exceptionally strong certainty.

Kant's weakness lies in the fact that he still accepts, if not in name yet in fact, principles or axioms, as truths that are immediately certain, while it is urged against Mill, that our certainty of axioms, so called, does not rest upon experience. No amount of past or additional experience makes them more certain, and in case experiences arise contradictory to them, we do not doubt our axioms, but distrust our observation.

The author of the article "Axiom" in the "Encyclopædia Britannica" (Prof. G. C. Robertson) still regards the question as unsettled. He says of the claims of these rival schools:

"The question being so perplexed no other course seems open than to try to determine the nature of axioms mainly upon such instances as are, at least practically, admitted by all, and these are mathematical principles."

Our solution of this perplexing problem is to regard the rules of reasoning, such as Euclid has formulated under the name of postulates, as products of rigidly formal reasoning.

Man's reasoning consists of his mental operations, and man's mental operations are acts.

The mere forms of mental acts are such as advancing step by step from a fixed starting-point. We thus create purely formal magnitudes. We can name every step and can combine two and more steps. This is not all. We can also revert step by step; we can disassociate our combinations and again separate our magnitudes partly or entirely into their elements. Purely mental acts are, as acts, not different from any other happenings in the world. The sole difference consists in their being conscious, and that for convenience sake a starting-point is fixed as an indispensable point of reference. The starting-point may be any point; the names of the products of our mental operations may be any names; yet it is requisite that, once taken, the point of reference shall remain the same, and also the names of the same magnitudes must remain the same.

Our mental operations, by which the rigidly formal products, commonly called *a priori*, are produced, being the given data out of which mind grows, and as regards their formal nature being the same as any other operations in the world, we say that the products of these operations are ultimately based upon experience. However, they are not experience in the usual (i.e. Kant's) sense of the word; they are not information received through the senses. They are due to the self-observation of the subject that experiences, and this self observation is something different from the mysterious intuition in which the intuitionists believe. The subject that experiences does not take note of external facts, but of its own acts, constructing general schedules of operations which hold good wherever the same operations are performed.

Thus on the one hand we deny that the rigidly formal truths are generalisations abstracted from innumerable observations; and on the other hand that they are axioms or self-evident truths, or principles acquired by some kind of immediate intuition. We recognise their universality and necessity for all kinds of operations that take place, and yet escape the mysticism that our surest and most reliable knowledge must be taken for granted, that it is unproved, unprovable and without any scientific warrant.

We have to devote special chapters to a further explanation of this view of the *a priori*, of the formal, and of the methods of pure thought or reason.

A PRIORI AND A POSTERIORI.

It is very doubtful whether the two terms, *a priori* and *a posteriori*, have been of more good than evil. Having gradually dropped the usage of Latin as the language of science and philosophy, we can at the present day, at any rate, do without them; we can replace them by more modern, more definite, and less obscure expressions, and it seems, thus, advisable to discard them. However, as they have played an important part in the history of philosophy, and as they are still much in vogue, we must understand them. As they are very expressive and concise, we may use them whenever they cannot be misinterpreted. At any rate we must know for what purposes they were coined, in what sense they have been used, properly and improperly, and by what modern terms they are to be replaced.

The terms were invented by scholastic philosophers, and are an attempt to translate the contrast between the order of things and the order of cognition, as described by Aristotle in the two phrases, "prior by nature," or $\pi\rho o\tau \varepsilon\rho o\nu$ $\tau\tilde{\eta}$ $\varphi\upsilon\sigma\varepsilon\iota$, and "prior to us," or $\pi\rho\acute{o}\tau\varepsilon\rho o\nu$ $\pi\rho\grave{o}s$ $\dot{\eta}\mu\tilde{\alpha}s$. Aristotle says:

"Prior is that which is nearer to a certain principle .... either according to place .... or time .... or order .... Some are according to reason, and some according to sense; for, certainly, according to reason, things that are universal are prior; but according to sense the singulars are prior."

Aristotle regards the general law or principle from which we explain a particular fact as logically prior; the former conditions the latter. In our experience, however, we confront single facts and rise from them by induction to the principles. Thus, what in nature appears to be first, is last in our mind, and what is first in our mind appears to be a mere application of the laws of nature.

During the thirteenth century the terms *a prioribus* and *a posterioribus*, were employed by Albertus Magnus, to denote respectively the methods of deductive reasoning, which starting from principles goes down to consequences, and of inductive reasoning which starts from single instances and rises up to general principles. Albert of Saxony in the fourteenth century used the terms *a priori* and *a posteriori* in the same sense as Albertus Magnus. And this usage was universally adopted and adhered to, until shortly before Kant the meaning of the terms was changed.

Leibnitz uses the term *a priori* as equivalent to pure reason, and Wolf says "that which we add to our knowledge by experience (*quod experiundo addiscimus*) is called *a posteriori*, that which becomes known to us by reasoning *a priori*."

Kant regarded this usage of the terms as popularly accepted. He says:

"If a man undermined his house, we say, 'he might have known *a priori* that it would have fallen,' that is, he needed not to have waited for the experience that it did actually fall."

Lambert, whose modes of thought exercised a strong influence upon Kant, says in the *Neue Organon*, §639, "only that can be called strictly and absolutely *a priori* which has nothing whatever to do with experience."

A priori and *a posteriori* were formerly applied to the two methods of reasoning. Lambert made them have reference to the products of reasoning, and Kant followed his example. He uses "*a priori*" to denote such knowledge "as is altogether independent of experience and of sensuous impressions."

Commenting upon the example of the man who undermined his house, Kant continues:

"But still, *a priori*, he could not know even this much. For, that bodies are heavy, and, consequently, that they fall when their supports are taken away, must have been known to him previously, by means of experience.

"By the term 'knowledge *a priori*,' therefore, we shall in the sequel understand, not such as is independent of this or that kind of experience, but such as is absolutely so of *all* experience. Opposed to this is empirical knowledge, or that which is possible only *a posteriori*, that is, through experience."

Kant makes a further distinction of pure and impure knowledge *a priori*. He says:

"Knowledge *a priori* is either pure or impure. Pure knowledge *a priori* is that with which no empirical element is mixed up. For example, the proposition, 'Every change has a cause,' is a proposition *a priori*, but impure, because change is a conception which can only be derived from experience."

The human intellect, according to Kant, is, even in an unphilosophical state, in possession of certain cognitions *a priori*; and he finds that the criterion of these *a priori* truths consists in their necessity and universality. Empirical cognition is neither necessary nor universal; we cannot declare that "it could not possibly be otherwise," and all we can say is, that "so far only as we have hitherto observed there is no exception to this or that rule." When we confront truths to which we have to attribute necessity and universality, Kant proposes to call them *a priori*.

Upon a closer investigation, Kant found that man is in possession of quite a number of such truths, to which universality and necessity are unhesitatingly attributed. They cover the whole domain of the formal sciences, of arithmetic and mathematics, including also the idea of causation and the purely formal modes of logical thought. All these truths, Kant argued, cannot have been derived from experience, for by experience we can never attain to necessity and universality. Moreover, experience becomes possible only on the supposition of these *a priori* truths. Only by conceiving sensations as effects, can we think of their causes as objective realities. Thus the ideas of causation and of all other *a priori* truths are the conditions of experience, and as such, as conditions of experience, they can, according to Kant, not be found in experience; they are prior to experience.

Kant does not (as is often imputed to him) understand the *a priori* in a temporal sense; his *a priori* is prior logically or according to reason. Yet he regards it as conditioned by and dependent upon the constitution of our minds.

Those ideas which as the condition of experience are prior to experience Kant calls "transcendental."

* * *

Kant regarded all purely *a priori* knowledge as empty, and all purely *a posteriori* experience as blind. Transcendental ideas have no other application than to the data of the *a posteriori*; and the *a posteriori* alone is a mere chaos of incoherent feelings.

The principles *a priori* constitute, as it were, the organ of cognition, which serves to give connection to our sense-impressions.

Kant's apriorism was free from mysticism, but the disciples of the great master looked with a certain awe upon the *a priori*, and regarded it as something that was not begotten in the natural way, but came into this world of ours through some mysterious spiritual channels. And Kant's unfortunate term, "transcendentalism," helped much to increase the mist in their minds. The term "transcendental" sounds very much like "transcendent," but while the former, in Kant's terminology, comprises the most lucid and indubitable truths, (viz., those of the formal sciences,) the latter denotes that which transcends all comprehension. In English, the term "transcendental" is not only similar in sound to, but is actually used as a synonym of, "transcendent," and, indeed, "transcendental" is a more common and more popular expression than "transcendent." Here is cause enough for confusion, and those who love confusion have not failed to avail themselves of this splendid opportunity.

It would lead us too far should we venture into the labyrinth of errors built by Kantians with the master's perplexing terminology. Moreover, it requires not a little trouble to trace all the mistakes to their various sources. Thus we are satisfied with a general warning and wish only to add that transcendentalism, in its post-Kantian editions (especially in the revised Oxford version of Prof. T. H. Green) is greatly interested in the demonstration of an ego, and the mysticism of the misconstrued meaning of the *a priori*, supplies for this the most imposing argument. For, surely, if the connection of the sense-impressions, which changes them into coherent experience, is furnished from the resources of the mind alone, the mind must be something radically different from the world, and the dualism of spirituality and materiality is firmly established.

The idea of an *a priori* is freighted with additional dangers. Every idea, to which any philosophising Tom, Dick, and Harry attributed necessity and generality, was declared to be of such an *a priori* nature, and thus it happened that any inveterate error established by tradition and instilled into the mind from early childhood, either actually was, or at least easily could be, sanctioned with a certain show of philosophical profundity. The *a priori* became a kind of special revelation and was employed as a reliable evidence of the supernatural. It was used as the cornerstone of dualism. And it was a source of constant worry to this class of Kantians that Kant himself had not only not drawn these consequences, but actually disavowed them. Kant had declared that the ego (the unity of the soul) was a mere paralogism, a fallacy, of pure reason. The unity of the soul, he said, is a mere synthesis.

* * *

No wonder that those who distrust the soundness of dualistic and mystical conclusions have acquired an aversion towards the very idea of the *a priori* and suspect it as a fraud. August Comte discards the *a priori* without any ado. To him, everything *a priori* is metaphysical. He and his school discredit all argumentation by pure reason as purely subjective and unwarranted.

Among English philosophers no one has denounced and ridiculed the *a priori* with more vigor than John

Stuart Mill. Like the French positivists, he stands on the principle of sensationalism, that all knowledge has been derived from sense-experience. To him the *a priori* is an unmitigated error and a philosophical superstition. He sees in it not the slightest inkling of truth.

Mr. Mill sets forth the motives that induced him to reject the *a priori* in his autobiography.

'There is not any idea, feeling, or power, in the human mind, which, in order to account for it, requires that its origin should be referred to any other source than experience.

"Whatever may be the practical value of a true philosophy of these matters, it is hardly possible to exaggerate the mischiefs of a false one. The notion that truths external to the mind may be known by intuition or consciousness, independently of observation and experience, is, I am persuaded, in these times the great intellectual support of false doctrines and bad institutions. By the aid of this theory every inveterate belief and every intense feeling, of which the origin is not remembered, is enabled to dispense with the obligation of justifying itself by reason, and is erected into its own all-sufficient voucher and justification."

Mr. Mill is justified in rejecting anything that cannot be reduced to experience, viz., experience in the sense in which we use the term. He is further justified in rejecting any theory or idea that claims to be true by intuition or consciousness. Unproved truths and axioms have no place in science or in the philosophy of science. But Mill rejects anything that cannot be reduced to sense-experience. He discards the *a priori*, and all that which, in Kant's sense is implied by the *a priori*, viz., necessity and universality. Mill went so far as to declare boldly that we could not know whether twice two will always and everywhere be four. It might be five in other parts of the universe. Together with the errors of Kantism he rejected its truths and attacked the latter not less impatiently than the former.

Such is the contrast that has been artificially produced between Empiricism and Apriorism; and there are many thinkers of weight to-day who believe that the differences of these two schools are irreconcilable.

* * *

Let us go back to Kant, for there is so much system about his thought that a criticism of his ideas will be the best method of setting us aright.

The main problem of the *a priori* and *a posteriori* is whether or not there is any knowledge to which we can rightfully attribute necessity and universality. This is tantamount to the problem, Does reality possess certain features which cannot be otherwise, but must be such as they are in any one of its parts? If there are such necessary and universal features, we can apply the knowledge thereof *a priori* to any possible experience, and these features, being something that is known even of otherwise unknown objects, will thus form the connecting link by which we can approach the unknown.

This is the old problem of mediæval Realism *versus* Nominalism. We cannot deny that the realists propounded many fantastic theories about the existence of universals, which to some of them appeared as entities or things in themselves; and Nominalism may be regarded as a wholesome reaction against the errors of Realism. Nevertheless, Realism was the sounder doctrine.

The formal sciences actually afford such information about things as can be *a priori* applied to any possible experience. Logical, mathematical, arithmetical principles are universal and necessary. And the question is only, whence does our knowledge of them come and how can we prove their universality and necessity?

These important questions were neither asked nor answered by Kant; he left them as a great blank in his theory, and this is the reason why his followers so easily drifted into mysticism.

Kant seems to assume that that faculty which connects, compares, and separates sensuous impressions exists independently of all experience; it only needs to be awakened or roused into activity. But it is obvious that it develops together with the increasing product of experience.

Kant's fundamental mistake in his premises is that he regards experience as a number of single sense-impressions which remain unconnected, yet there can be no doubt about it that they are naturally connected in every organism. Every sense-impression leaves a trace, and all succeeding sense-impressions leave other traces, and all these traces blend, or become otherwise associated among themselves. Our sensations are as naturally arranged into a system as are our limbs into an organism; and there is no need of assuming the existence of a special connecting faculty.

Kant overlooks the fact that there is form and coherence in the world of objects, and that the human mind is in possession of the conditions by which it can construct all kinds of formal combinations, and that these conditions are parts, not only of the mind's existence but of existence in general.

Sense-impressions are not without form. The sense-impression of a rose is not merely a sensuous impression, it possesses also a definite form, and several sense-impressions are not isolated single phenomena, but inter-related events. Form and interrelation are objective qualities, which are imported into the mind by experience, and distinguished from the purely sensory elements by abstraction.

There is a peculiar contrast between the formal and the sensory elements of experience. The formal is empty of contents. Its entire substance consists of mere relations, and when we construct in our mind such empty relations, so as to note the conditions which they constitute, the materials of our investigation are complete. We need not wait for additional information from other sources. Thus our knowledge of the product of every special construction is, in its way, exhaustive, and we can proceed systematically.

THE METHODS OF PHILOSOPHY.

The intrinsic emptiness of the purely formal implies a sameness of its nature, all differences being due to construction. The sameness, found in the *a priori*, implies the universality of its laws, which means that the same constructions are always and everywhere the same. As they are in one case, so they are in all cases. The result is rigidly and unequivocally determined. They furnish us with methods, schedules of reference, and plans which like blanks have to be filled out.

* * *

The terms *a priori* and *a posteriori* may still be popularly used in the scholastic sense, the former as a reasoning from a general principle to its consequences, the latter from single instances to a general principle. In philosophy they denote the formal and the material; and the formal sciences (arithmetic, mathematics, logic, etc.), offering systematic statements of universal application, constitute the organ and the condition of all scientific experience. There is no science without counting, or measuring, or classification.

The problem of the *a priori* (or rather of man's ability to know something beforehand concerning the subjects of his investigation, even concerning those which he never as yet has met with in experience) is the most fundamental problem of philosophy. It lurks everywhere, and no philosophy can avoid it. It is the cornerstone of the other problem, How is knowledge possible?

The data of our experience are single sense-impressions; how can they be changed into a system of knowledge which may be used as a guide for future experience?

This is the basic problem of philosophy, and this was Kant's problem. It may be difficult to understand the solution of Kant's problem, but it seems to us not difficult to understand the problem itself and also the inevitableness of the problem.

* * *

Prof. J. G. Schurman presents in *The Philosophical Review* for March, 1893, a very lucid exposition of "Kant's Critical Problem." It is remarkable, however, that he does not recognise its true nature. He says:

"For my own part I am not more certain of a demonstration of Euclid than of a chemist's analysis of water into hydrogen and oxygen."

While we may not be more certain about the correctness of a mathematical demonstration than about the truth of the statement of a chemical analysis, we ought to know that the nature of these two operations are radically different. The former is a mental construction, which, if correct, is applicable to any experience; the latter is the statement of a group of experiences, which, if it appropriately describes them, is called true. We know the former to be correct, because we made it ourselves. We know the latter to be true, because we saw it, or observed it. The problem is, How can the products of purely mental construction (even those into which no elements of a knowledge by experience enter) be applicable to experience, and this is a problem which demands an answer. It is a problem which was and is still overlooked or misunderstood by the English school, represented by Locke, Hume, Mill, and the great bulk of modern thinkers.

Professor Schurman regards the problem as conditioned by "the rationalism which shaped all Kant's speculations—a dogmatism boasting a rational knowledge of things without the aid of sense-experience." Thus it is in his opinion "not merely obsolete, but so unintelligible that, without reading into it an esoteric meaning, it is often difficult to justify the composition of the 'Critique'."

Professor Schurman adds:

"Whoever, therefore, denies the universality and necessity of judgments, whether the so-called *vérités de fait* or the *vérités de raison* must find Kant's 'Critique' in large part superfluous and irrelevant."

Certainly, he who denies the universality and necessity of the *vérités de raison* must find Kant's "Critique" superfluous and irrelevant. This is Mill's position. He actually denied the universality and necessity of even such a statement as $2 \times 2 = 4$. But is there any one who would take the consequences of Mill's view seriously? The fact remains that all our science is built upon the conceptions of universality and necessity. Take away our trust in universality and necessity, and we can draw no conclusions whatever. We could not formulate our experiences in general laws, we should be confronted with single experiences only and be not entitled to suppose them to contain any other than accidental uniformities.

The fact remains, that the so-called "dogmatism boasting of a rational knowledge without the aid of sense-experience" does form the basis of all our sciences. There is no sense-experience in counting and measuring, there is no sense-experience in a syllogism nor in any purely formal operations of reason; and yet we apply them. Why can they be applied? That is the question.

The truths of reason (although in themselves mere empty forms) are the cement of our knowledge. Deny their universality and necessity and you make knowledge impossible. But if knowledge were unreliable, if its reliability were merely a happy incident, man's very existence, his reason, his rational soul, his humanity would become an insolvable problem.

* * *

The terms *a priori* and *a posteriori* have been used to approach the fundamental problem of philosophy demanding an explanation of the question, How is reason (or rational knowledge) at all possible?

Thought is not sensation. Thought is the interaction that takes place among sensations or the memories of sensations. Thought is not possible and would never have risen into being without the sense-material furnished by the senses. But thought does not consist of the sense-material. Thought is the formal, the relational elements in the minds of sentient beings.

That body of truths which Kant called *a priori* we prefer to call "formal knowledge." A denial of the existence or applicability of that which in Kant's awkward terminology is called *a priori*, i. e. a denial of formal knowledge, is tantamount to a denial of the existence and applicability of reason.

Whatever Kant's errors may have been in the solution of the problem, he was right in his statement of the fact that there is *a priori* knowledge. Kant says in the preface to his "Critique of Practical Reason" (a passage which Professor Schurman quotes without seeing its strength):

"What worse could happen to these our efforts than that somebody should make the unexpected discovery that there is no *a priori* knowledge at all, and can be none. But there is no ground for anxiety. That would be to prove by *reason that there is no reason*. For we say that we know anything by reason only when we are conscious that we could have known it, even if it had not been given us in experience; so that knowledge through reason and knowledge *a priori* are the same."

THE FORMAL.

Science begins with the application of formal thought, viz., with counting, measuring, and classifying. Only with the assistance of the formal sciences can we master the material given in the sensory data of experience; and thus it happens that the formal is the condition, not of any kind of experience, but of all systematic experience.

The formal sciences are the tools of cognition. That to which they cannot be applied remains unexplained.

* * *

The different formal sciences are constructions of a purely formal nature. Thus, numbers are a system of units (i. e. empty forms); the logical categories a system of ideas, representing the various relations that can obtain among things, etc. These and other systems of pure forms do not exist ready-made, or in a latent form in the mind, but must be constructed out of the purely formal elements obtained from experience by abstraction.

Animals are incapable of making abstractions, and that is the reason why they cannot develop formal thought. Abstraction is the condition of the evolution of formal thought, for all the formal sciences move in a definite sphere of abstraction.

We have to distinguish between the rigidly formal,

the purely formal, and the empirically formal. The last kind of formality comprises the real forms of things with which we become acquainted in experience. The purely formal is to be found in the laws of stereometry, Euclidean geometry, etc., while logic, arithmetic, and algebra are rigidly formal.

What is the difference? The rigidly formal is the product of mental operations alone. Our mental activity alone is given. Otherwise there is no assumption whatever; no hypothesis, no axiom. In arithmetic we count our mental acts, we add and subtract them; and out of these operations the magnificent structure of this great formal science is created. We construct and observe the products of our construction. There is nothing but certain mental acts and the consequences involved in these acts. In all the rigidly formal sciences we combine and separate and recombine. By investing the same products with same names and equating the outcome of two sets of operations with the same results, we create the material of our science ourselves, as the spider spins the web that is to serve him as his field of operations, out of his own being. Says an old rhymster:

> "*Logicus araneæ potest comparari*
> *Quæ subtiles didicit telas operari,*
> *Quæ suis visceribus volunt consummari*
> *Et pretium musca si forte queat laqueari.*" *
>
> —Tom Wright, "Political Songs of England," p. 209.

* The logician may be compared to a spider who has learned to weave fine webs, which will be produced from her bowels, and the reward is a fly if she haply can catch one.

Mathematics and pure mechanics are not quite so rigidly *a priori* as arithmetic and algebra. Their constructions introduce some additional features which may be called assumptions or axioms, or derivations from experience, or common notions.

Whatever we may call them, they are arbitrary; they do not result as a necessary consequence from the operations with which we start.

While in the construction of rigidly formal sciences we have no choice left, we find that in the purely formal sciences there are several constructions possible. In Euclidean geometry, for instance, we execute, at the suggestion of the real space-conditions that surround us, one peculiar construction, because this special kind of geometry is most serviceable to us; but there are other possibilities left, and we can imagine analogous geometries built by the same mental operations but starting from other suppositions.

Euclidean geometry is a construction in which, through one point to a given straight line, one parallel only can be drawn. We can, however, construct other kinds of geometry in which, through a point to a given straight line, either no parallel at all or several parallels can be drawn.* Besides our tridimensional space

---

* The latter assumption, viz., that through a point to a straight line several parallels can be drawn will produce a space of negative curvature, while the former assumption admits of two possibilities, either two straight lines enclose a space (as, for instance, on the sphere) or two straight lines do not enclose a space—which produces elliptic geometry so-called, first observed by Klein. It is doubtful which case Riemann had in mind. (Translated from a private letter of Professor Lindemann in which he kindly gave a brief exposition of the situation.)

we can conceive of four, five, and n-dimensional spaces, and can with perfect precision define all the qualities which such spaces and their bodies must possess.

It is a matter of course that as soon as we have created, by some arbitrary construction, a certain feature in a formal system, we have to stick to it and take all its consequences. When we speak of triangles of Euclidean space, we cannot attribute to them the qualities of triangles in Lobatschewsky's or Riemann's space. Each geometry forms an independent domain for itself. None of them is truer than the other; and none of them should be confounded with the other.

The term "rigidly formal" is narrower than "purely formal." All rigidly formal truths are at the same time purely formal, but not all purely formal statements are rigidly formal.

*   *   *

Modern geometry proves that our notion of space is not rigidly formal; it is only purely formal. The statement that real space is tridimensional is not a necessary product of our mental operations. It is not on one and the same level with the statement $2 \times 2 = 4$. The latter is intrinsically necessary. There is no other possibility left. 2×2 will always be the same, and whatever we have called it, so we shall have to call it again, or at any rate regard it as equivalent and equal. Space, however, for all we know *a priori*, might be four or five or n-dimensional; and whether or not the world-space, i. e. the form of reality, is tridimensional is a matter of experience. Thus the statement, real space is tridimensional, contains an empirical or *a posteriori* element. It does not contain any information about the material world, the information it conveys is purely formal still, but it is not rigidly formal. It cannot be proposed as the only possible condition of being, for there are other constructions possible and imaginable. Tridimensional space is one instance only among innumerable possibilities, and we have through experience from *a posteriori* arguments sufficient reasons to believe (or if you prefer, to be assured) that this one instance is realised in the actual world in which we live.

Assuming then, from *a posteriori* arguments, that world-space is tridimensional, we can forthwith *a priori* apply to it all the laws of tridimensional space. All the various systems of Euclidean and non-Euclidean geometry, of mathematical or any other imaginable space-constructions are purely formal notions. But they are not the inevitable consequence of our mental operations only, they contain, each system its own peculiar conditions, which are arbitrarily established. Their character is not necessary, but might be otherwise.

Arbitrary constructions of such a nature have been called "axioms" and are now commonly called "assumptions." The one term is as bad as the other. The name "axiom" suggests that there are indubitable but unprovable truths, and the word "assumption" implies that we take some supposition for granted which may not be correct. We might assume the impossible or that which is contradictory to the consequences of the operations with which we start. We might assume that 2×2 is sometimes 4 and sometimes 5. The word assumption suggests the idea that our procedure is unfounded. We have neither to accept any truth without proof, nor are we allowed to make assumptions. Employing the mental functions which we possess, we can construct; and there is a choice, whether to construct a plane geometry or other geometries. But a choice is no assumption.

*   *   *

If the difference between the rigidly formal and the purely formal had been kept in mind by modern mathematicians, much confusion and many errors rising out of confusion would have been avoided. It has been said, for instance, that we do not know whether or not the sum of the angles in a plane triangle is exactly 180°; it may be somewhat more or less. They grant that it is very approximately so and declare that even the greatest triangles we can measure are too small to discover the deviation. As instances parallaxes of stars have been adduced, which make measurements on triangles whose sides sweep through cosmic space over the whole stellar universe; but it is a pity for this class of geometers that such deviations

as are found in these calculations keep within the reasonable limits of errors which occur in all analogous cases of observation. True, that among about forty measurements two only come out negative. That might be an argument in favor of a slightly curved space; but we can surmise that many other negative measurements have been suppressed as obviously erroneous.*
This view is based upon a misconception of the nature of the formal sciences.

A modern geometer may deny that world-space is tridimensional, but he cannot deny without inconsistency that the sum of the angles in a plane triangle is 180 degrees, for it is so by construction and cannot be otherwise unless we reverse the conditions upon which we have made the construction.

Suppose we construct a circle and propose the theorem that in a circle all the peripheral angles upon equal cords are equal, intending to prove that this follows with necessity from the qualities of the circle. Having done so a geometrical friend of ours steps in and denies the validity of the argument. He says, "The peripheral angles on equal cords in a circle as large as the orbit of the earth round the sun are approximately but not exactly equal. Your theorem may be right within certain limits and will be sufficient for all the small circles which occur in our practical experience. But whether it holds good generally is very doubtful still. In order to know that, we shall have

* *The Monist*, Vol. I, No. 2, p. 173-174.

to make more exact measurements with circles as large as the milky way. Within a century our children will probably know more about it than we do now with the insufficient material at our disposal."

What would we tell him? We should tell him that a circle remains a circle as much as a plane triangle remains a plane triangle; astronomy may prove that the orbit of the earth round the sun is only approximately a circle (celestial bodies move in conic sections, our earth moving nearly in a circle), but it can as little prove that peripheral angles on equal cords are only approximately equal, as the measurement of parallaxes can induce us to believe that the sum of plane triangles is only approximately not exactly equal to 180°.

Suppose that the parallaxes of stars really showed that these world-sized triangles of astronomy really and regularly measured somewhat more or less than 180°, what would be the conclusion? Would we indeed have to revise our mathematics and declare that mathematics is only approximately true? No, we should conclude that the rays of light do not travel in exactly straight lines, that their path is only approximately straight. However, whether or not the rays of light travel in straight lines is not a purely formal question at all; it is an empirically formal question, which has as little to do with pure mathematics as the question whether apples are exact or only approximate globes.

Important as is the difference between the rigidly formal and the purely formal (a difference entirely overlooked by Kant), the difference between the purely formal and the empirically formal is greater still. It is so obvious, however, that it has scarcely ever escaped attention and has led to the well known distinctions between purely formal mathematics, mechanics, logic, etc., and applied mathematics, mechanics, logic, etc. The purely formal sciences exclude all the incidental deviations of real objects, while the applied formal sciences take notice of them, introducing them as factors in their calculations.

How near Kant came to the solution of the problem which actually explains all and is in our opinion the only satisfactory answer possible, viz., that *the formal sciences are purely formal constructions*, will be seen from the following passage in Kant's preface to the second edition of his "Critique of Pure Reason."

"A new light must have flashed on the mind of the first man (*Thales*, or whatever may have been his name) who demonstrated the properties of the *isosceles* triangle. For he found that it was not sufficient to meditate on the figure, as it lay before his eyes, or the conception of it, as it existed in his mind, and thus endeavour to get at the knowledge of its properties, but that it was necessary to produce these properties, as it were, by a positive *a priori construction*; and that, in order to arrive with certainty at *a priori* cognition, he must not attribute to the object any other properties than those which necessarily followed from that which he had himself, in accordance with his conception, placed in the object."

After this explanation Kant falls back upon the theory that the *a priori* or purely formal elements are *given* by the mind, which is quite another thing than *constructed* by the mind. If they were "given by the mind" they would exist in the mind as a latent knowledge, in the same way that we know many things of which we are not conscious and to recollect which may require considerable mental effort. But if they are constructed by the mind, we need only look upon certain mental operations as given. The products of these operations are the object of the formal sciences. And in this way we can indeed escape all the perplexing consequences of Kant's transcendentalism.

*
* *

Kant was puzzled that we could know anything *a priori* concerning the constitution of things. He saw only two possibilities; either, he said, we have derived this knowledge from the things by experience, or we ourselves have put it into the things to which it really does not belong. The former possibility being excluded, since the purely formal truths are *a priori*, Kant accepted the other horn of the dilemma declaring that our faculty of cognition did not conform to the objects, but contrariwise, that the objects conform to cognition. The objects do not in themselves possess form, but our mind is so constituted that it cannot help attributing form and everything formal to the objects of our experience.

Kant did not see that form might be a property of all existence that, in that case, the purely formal in things would be of the same nature as the purely formal in man's mind.

Nature is throughout activity, and so our existence is throughout activity. Nature is constantly combining and separating; and these same operations are inalienable functions of our mind. They are given together with our existence.

When we construct some purely formal configuration with our nature-given mental operations, it will be the same as any other construction which has been made in the same way, be it in the domain either of things or of other minds. Nature performs the same operations which appear in man's mental activity. Being a part of existence, what is more natural than that man's bodily and mental existence partakes of the same form as all the other parts of the world that surrounds him.

A great and important part of our knowledge consists of rigidly formal theorems; they are *a priori*. And these rigidly formal theorems contain actual information concerning the real world. And why? Because they are systematic reconstructions of a certain feature of reality by operations which take place throughout the universe. When Kant says: Our mind "dictates" certain laws to the objects of experience; he uses a wrong expression or takes a poetical license seriously. The mind "dictates" nothing to reality. Reality is independent of what we think it to be. That which Kant calls dictating is a mere determining, a mere foretelling or predicting by constructing in our mind an analogous model.

The agreement between our model and reality proves only that the model is correct, it does not prove that the model does any dictating. The model dictates as little to reality as a barometer dictates what air-pressure there is to be in the atmosphere.

The purely formal gives information concerning things so general that they are the same throughout the universe, and the rigidly formal concerning things so universal that they are the same in all possible universes.

THE PROBLEM OF THE THREE DIMENSIONS OF SPACE.

OUR geometricians have always attempted to construct space from its simplest elements. They take a point which is very vaguely defined as that which has neither parts nor magnitude. The point is moved, and its path is called a line. Now, a peculiar difficulty arises, when out of moving points alone they propose to define the idea of straightness. This is impossible, and, in want of anything better, a straight line is generally defined as the shortest distance between two points. Having a straight line, the rest is easy enough. We construct a plane by moving a straight line in any direction not its own, and solids, again, by moving a plane in any direction not contained in the plane.

Many attempts have been made to circumvent the difficulty of presenting an unequivocal and purely rational, i. e., rigidly formal or *a priori*, definition of a straight line. Vain as these attempts were for that purpose, they have not been futile, for they have led to the startling discovery of the possibility of other space constructions. It is strange, nevertheless, that no one has yet called attention to the faults of the method itself. Should we succeed in satisfactorily defining or constructing a straight line, it would avail us nothing. We should be in the predicament of the physician who has removed one symptom only of a disease, without curing its deeper-seated cause, which continues to work evil effects in other parts of the organism.

* * *

The fault of the geometrical method lies (so it seems to me) in its apriorism. It is the same vice as that of the ontological school of philosophy, which starts the world from nothing. Nothing is one minus one ($0 = 1 - 1$), which, when transposed, reads $0 + 1 = 1$. This at once launches us into positive statements. True philosophy, however, must not only start from facts, but also be and remain a statement of facts. Philosophy is the science of the method of dealing with facts according to their nature. The method of dealing with facts has to be derived from the facts them-

THE METHODS OF PHILOSOPHY. 91

selves. Pure reason is nothing, unless it is the interaction of ideas. All processes of reasoning are mental operations with representations of facts. They start from known facts and proceed to unknown facts; and if the conclusions at which we arrive are not facts, our reasoning is a mere Vanity Fair.

All the formal sciences, not less than philosophy, must start with something; they must be based upon facts, and the facts of the formal sciences are the operations which are constitutional to our mind, and without which nothing would exist. In mathematics the additional fact of space is presupposed, mathematics being the science of purely formal space-relations.

* * *

How lame is the old method of constructing space with points!

First, notice that the definition of a point is negative. A point is something without parts and magnitude. Are there not many things without parts and magnitude, which are not points? All material things have parts and magnitude, but immaterial things have no extension and cannot always be divided into parts. Has, for instance, the color red any parts? Has a pain any parts? A desire may be great or strong, but it cannot be large. An idea may be grand, but it can possess no magnitude. Or can any one state what are the size and the parts of the idea of unity?

Second, consider that space, the thing to be constructed, is after all, tacitly or even openly, presupposed. To obviate the first objection an amendment is made. "A point," we are told, "is that *in space* which has neither parts nor magnitude." * If space is presupposed, why trouble at all to construct it?

Having constructed the solid as the third power of extension, we suddenly stop; for space has, so we say, three dimensions only. This seems arbitrary and our mathematicians are puzzled as to why we cannot continue constructing four, five, or n-dimensional bodies. That such constructions are, theoretically, quite admissible, Grassmann's, Lobatschewsky's, and Riemann's investigations have demonstrated.

* * *

Suppose we begin at the other end and say that in mathematics (1) our *mental operations*, and (2) *space* are given. Our mathematical operations are acts that take place in space; they are motions, and space is the possibility of motion.

Points are not real objects, but mental artifices to determine a position in space. A point is *in* space, but it is not *of* space, which means, it indicates a location, but has no extension. We may use as a point, or indicator of a special spot, anything we please, our own body, our finger, the point of a pencil, a dot, the whole earth, the sun, or Sirius. But we have to bear in mind that, extension being excluded, we have, as a

---

* Most of the German text-books offer the following definition: *Ein Punkt ist ein Ding 'im Raum,' das keine Theile hat.*

matter of mental abstraction, to ignore the materiality of these indicators of location, and in case they are as large as, for instance, Sirius, we have to know where to locate the point, either in its centre, or at some specially marked corner.

Points are conceived as movable; and "space" being the condition of motion, we have further to inquire into the nature of space. We can construct various kinds of mathematical space, such as planes, homaloidal (or even) as well as curved, the three-dimensional space for stereometrical constructions, and also imaginary spaces of n dimensions. Yet we find, as a matter of experience, that our world-space is three-dimensional, and here we ask, Could not space just as well have either more or less than three dimensions? Is the tridimensionality of space purely arbitrary, or can we detect for it any assignable reason?

Certainly, considering *a priori* arguments alone, space—i. e., the real world-space—could have any number of dimensions, or no existence at all, just as we do not know why the world exists, and why there is not in its place mere nothingness.

* * *

The dimensions of space would appear less arbitrary, and we should sooner acquiesce in their nature, if they were infinite in number. Infinitude is the absence of limits. Infinitude, accordingly, is a matter of course, while the finitude of a certain limit or number is a special restriction, which calls for a special explanation.

In the same way, eternity, or infinitude of time, is a matter of course, if but existence be given, while beginning and end must have their special causes. Eternity is implied in existence.

We ought to expect space to be in possession of infinite dimensions, for such a state of things would be as plausible and as little startling as the eternity of time.

This consideration suggests the idea of how to construct a space, not as Riemann did, of n (viz., any number of) dimensions, but of truly infinite (viz., inexhaustibly many) dimensions.

While attempting to think a space of an infinite number of dimensions, we are struck by the fact that space actually possesses infinite—not dimensions, but —directions.

A space of infinite directions is that condition of motion in which there is no restriction whatever. It means the absence of any impediment.

* * *

What is the difference between a dimension and a direction?

Directions are the possibilities of motion in actual space; dimensions, however, are contrivances for determining directions as well as locations in space from a given reference point. Directions, accordingly, must be considered as given by nature; they are data of experience, and, being infinite in number, they are exactly what we must expect them to be. Dimensions are artificial; dimensions, as such, are not given by nature. They are as little natural as right angles, or logarithms, or a sine, or an integral, or an infinitesimal.

Straight lines are directions of a peculiar kind. They possess a simplicity and consistency which distinguishes them from irregular lines and from curves.

* * *

Sir Robert Stawell Ball, of Cambridge, England, speaking of the theories of some modern mathematicians, who deny the Euclidean axiom of parallel lines, and proposing the theory that a straight line, after a journey which is not infinite in its length, may return to its starting-point, says, in an article published in the *Fortnightly Review*, May, 1893, p. 632 :

"If any one should think this a difficulty, I would recommend him to try to affix a legitimate definition to the word 'straight.' He will find that the strictly definable attributes of straightness are quite compatible with the fact that a particle moving along a straight line will ultimately be restored to the point from which it departed."

Sir Robert Ball does not believe in homaloidal space, such as is presupposed by Euclid, but thinks that if he could but make space a little bit curved, all such difficulties, as infinitude, would vanish.

Now, we believe that the straightness which constitutes the homaloidality of space is not so much a quality of space, as of our methods of calculating and computing space-relations.

We can imagine a condition of things in which, through some unknown cause, a point moving with strictest consistency in one and the same direction should suffer a slight, but constant, switching off. This would make Euclidean straight lines no longer available for certain practical purposes, but would not render them theoretically impossible; nor would it involve homaloidal geometry in contradictions. The infinitude of homaloidal space would remain what it is now, a difficulty, but not an antinomy. However, the finitude of a curved space presents innumerable new problems, a satisfactory solution of which appears very improbable.

Professor Ball says that all the strictly definable attributes of straightness are compatible with curved space. While granting the difficulty of defining straightness by purely *a priori* methods from moving points only, we claim that straight lines are describable by methods of abstraction on the ground of our space-experiences.

Take two points of any line, and turn the line between the points round itself. Every line which by this operation will change its place is called curved, while that line which remains in its place is called straight; in other words, every curved line has an axis of rotation outside itself, while the straight line is its own axis of rotation. In one case, rotation makes a difference, in the other case, rotation does not involve change of position ; and this latter condition is what Euclid calls "even," in describing a straight line.* We do not intend to attach too much importance to this description of straightness, but it seems to fulfil all the demands—except that it leaves space as infinite as before, which, however, ought to be expected.

We must not forget that infinitude, being the absence of limits, is a simpler conception than finitude. While the infinitude of space involves difficulties, the finitude of space, so it seems to us, involves not only an innumerable host of undreamed of problems, but also an actual antinomy. On close inspection it will be found to be a paralogism of reason.

*   *   *

Straight lines, as peculiar paths of motion, remind us of rays of light. Light is the quickest motion we know of ; and the problem has often been proposed, Why do rays of light travel in straight lines, i. e., in paths of shortest time?

Physicists of former ages found in this condition of things an argument for the Creator's wisdom ; and at present there is a tendency to regard the path of a ray of light as the prototype of straight lines in geom-

---

* Euclid says : "A straight line is that which lies evenly between its extreme points."

etry. The fact, however, is that light does not travel in straight lines or on paths of shortest time, but in all directions and on an infinite number of paths. But on the paths of shortest time the action of light is so intensified as to produce that peculiar result which we call rays.

Similarly, if we consider a point as a permanent source of a homogeneous motion, which simultaneously takes place in all its infinite directions, the continuous summation of the results in the paths of shortest time would mark the geometrical straight line. This should assist us in looking upon the nature of a straight line as the accumulated sum of motion in one and the same direction. Suppose that motion pours forth in all directions, and that every point to which the motion is transferred is again a source of motion in all directions: Among the infinite number of directions there is always one which continues the direction from which the motion is received, so as to connect it directly, i. e., on the shortest path, with the original source. Thus the straight line represents the maximum of action in a minimum of absolutely unimpeded motion, and must as such be taken as a *Grenzbegriff*, i. e., a conception which denotes the utmost limit to be reached by a certain operation.

The homaloidality (or evenness) of space is not a positive but a negative quality, being due to the non-existence of any impediment of motion, it means the absence of positive qualities.

Suppose a ray of light did not travel in a straight line, we should not have to infer that space is curved but that there is an impediment to the action of light, preventing it from reaching the limit of a maximum of action in a minimum of time. Part of the action being absorbed by the resistance of the medium through which it travels the ray is no longer straight, but curved.

Suppose that a rotating line could not be made identical with its axis of rotation we should then have to assign a cause for our inability to reach the limit of its shortest size.

If the straight line is viewed as a *Grenzbegriff*, the mystery which surrounds it disappears. We need no longer marvel either at the wisdom of the Creator that rays of light travel in paths of shortest time, or at the arbitrariness of nature that space is homaloidal.

* * *

The problem accordingly is not, why is a straight line not curved, but what is a straight line? And concerning the extension of space, we must not ask why is space three-dimensional, but why can the infinite directions of space be reduced for purposes of space-determination or for the location of points to three orthogonal directions.

This problem is not a problem of philosophy proper, but of the algebra of formal thought, and we are not as yet prepared to solve it. We must be satisfied at present to have formulated it. Suffice it here to indicate that we are inclined to believe that any infinitude may for practical measurements always be reduced to three fundamental elements, the first one of which may be selected arbitrarily, while the second is to be constructed with reference to the first, and the third with reference to the first and second.*

Suppose we have a system of infinitely various interrelations. We represent them graphically as an infinite number of points in all possible positions, all of which are combined among themselves by lines. It is inevitable that the elements of these interconnections will be triplet relations. Suppose that all points are interconnected, the diagram will consist of triangles only. Every elementary interrelation will be of a threefold nature and is determinable by three magnitudes.

We can always, with triads, or, so to speak, with logical triangles, compute any relation in any universe of infinite possibilities. Those interrelations which are more complex (we might call them polyads or polygonal relations) can always be resolved into or reduced to triads or triplet-relations.

*   *   *

Those who have studied Hegel are familiar with the importance of the trinity-relation. The logical necessity of the triad is inevitable, for every simple relation is

---

* In this connection we call attention to the fact that the innumerable varieties of color-tints can be reduced to, and determined by, three fundamental colors.

inevitably triune in its nature. The relation A and B is not a duality, but a trinity, for besides A and B we have that which combines them or constitutes their peculiar connection. Thus it is a logical necessity that all dualism leads to triism or rather triunism, and triunism is again monism.

We cannot even conceive of God without attributing trinity to him. An absolute unity would be non-existence. God, if thought of as real and active, involves an antithesis, which may be formulated as God and World, or *natura naturans* and *natura naturata*, or in some other way. This antithesis implies already the trinity-conception. When we think of God not only as that which is eternal and immutable in existence, but also as that which changes, grows, and evolves, we cannot escape the result and we must progress to a triune God-idea. The conception of a God-Man, of a Saviour, of God revealed in evolution, brings out the antithesis of God Father and God Son, and the very conception of this relation implies God the Spirit that proceeds from both.

Mathematics is a constructive science and we expect to find only *a priori* constructions in it. But this is a mistake. Although mathematics is a constructive science, it starts from certain data, and the data of mathematics are not the products of *a priori* constructions, but the results of abstraction.

Mathematical space, too, is rather an abstraction than a construction. We first drop in our thoughts the materiality as well as the dynamical reality of relations and retain the mere form of interrelations—viz., positions and directions. These positions and directions are then taken to be infinite and continuous; and for purposes of determination they are reduced to the three coördinates, called dimensions.

Our explanations must not attempt to bridge the gap from non-existence to existence. We must not attempt to elucidate the qualities of that which exists from that which does not exist. Our explanations must aspire to be systematic descriptions of that which is, and comprehension consists in recognising the consistency of being. That existence exists, and that it is not non-existence will always impress us as arbitrary, but the qualities of existence will cease to appear arbitrary when we find that any one fact agrees with all other facts. The quality α which we find in the configuration A appears different from β which we find in the configuration B. But when we find that R or Reality under the peculiar conditions given in A appears as α and under the peculiar conditions given in B appears as β, so that $\alpha = RA$ and $\beta = RB$, we cease to consider α and β as arbitrary.

The tridimensionality of space strikes us as arbitrary, but its main arbitrariness is the arbitrariness of reality itself. Yet, above all this there is hope that we can conceive it as a consistent corollary of the infinitude of space-relations. We can regard it as due to the same reason that a syllogism, consisting of two premises and one conclusion, presents a triad relation. In that case the tridimensionality of space is in the same predicament as other facts which can be explained by the usual methods. It is neither more nor less arbitrary than, for instance, the value of π as $3.14589\ldots$ and of logarithm 3 as 0.4771213.

REASON.

The difference between the two great philosophical parties of the middle ages may, in a modernised form, be characterised as follows:

The Realist recognises forms as realities of a universal nature. The samenesses in the world, the similarities and dissimilarities, the relations and the changes taking place in these relations, are actual and objective. Thus the universal is real.

The Nominalist regards universals as idealities. He professes to know only single experiences and believes that he is not warranted in assuming a coherence among them. To him the samenesses which a mind discovers are not real; they are mental impositions. The regularities of laws have no objective existence, but are purely subjective conceptions, and universals are mere names.

To the Realist the universe is one whole, the bond of union being the universal in the single experiences.

To the Nominalist the universe is a sum of innumerable items, and we are not entitled to make any conclusion from the nature of one of them as to the nature of others.

The nominalistic position appears to be the more guarded one. But when adhered to and applied with consistency it makes knowledge impossible. It is in its root scepticism and leads to agnosticism.

Now the question is, can the realistic assumption be proved or not? Is the denial of the legitimacy of realistic conclusions justifiable or not?

If the universe were actually an indifferent medley of single facts, without any coherence of their own, so that all the order we see in the world were given to it by ourselves, reality would be more correctly pictured in the animal brain than in the human mind.

The question, as to whether or not there is any universality, is the problem of reason. If there were no universality there would be no dependence on reason. Reason would be of a purely ideal, or merely subjective and illusory, nature. Its application to reality would be an assumption, at best a mere working hypothesis. Thus there would be no knowledge, but opinions only, and we could, with strict consistency, not even say that if all men are mortal, Caius, being a man, must be mortal, too.

When we deny universality, we kill reason, for universality is the life-blood of reason.

How can we justify the assumption of universality?

There may be some coherence among the many single facts of our experience, but perhaps we are unable to verify it, and, for all we know, the coherence may be partial.

Before we enter into a discussion of the problem, let us ask: Is it at all true that experience consists of many single items, and do we not, when treating experience as such, inadvertently imply a whole theory, the consequence of which will crop out unawares afterwards? It may be true that realism begins with an assumption, but we should not be blind to the fact that nominalism also is not free of assumptions.

The truth is that experience is a coherent entirety, and the existence of single facts is due only to an analysis of experience. There is no fact unconnected with other facts, and the connections of facts are not merely incidental features. Reality can be understood only when it is conceived as a system of changes. Events are intelligible only when viewed as transformations, so that the laws of form which obtain in these transformations are universal.

Thus it appears that universality is as much a fact of experience as are sensations. Sensation is the subjective symbol for what objectively appears as matter, and the connections and forms of our sensations are the subjective aspect of the interrelations of material reality. The truth is, that not only matter is real, but its forms, also.

The problem of universality is the same as the problem of necessity, and the problem of necessity is the problem of determinableness. How is it that we can determine certain things?* This again is the problem of reason.

The most perplexing feature of reason is its faculty of *a priori* determination. We can make certain statements with perfect assurance concerning things which sometimes we cannot even know by direct experience.

For instance, we accurately measure first the distance between two observatories, which happen to lie in the same longitude, and then the two angles at which the moon passes through the meridian. We thus have a triangle of which one side and the two adjacent angles are known, and it is easy enough to calculate from these data the distance of the moon from the earth. We can never directly measure the moon's distance by yard-sticks or tape-lines, but we can, without further experience or experiment, be sure that calculation as such is reliable. The moon's distance being known, we can proceed to measure the sun's distance by measuring the angle at which sun and moon appear on earth when the moon is exactly at the half. We again have a triangle in which three parts are known, viz., (1) the distance between earth and moon; (2) the angle at the moon as a right angle; and (3) the angle at the earth by measurement. And from these data we can calculate the hypothenuse of

---

* Necessity is often regarded as a compulsion, and determinism is accordingly confounded with fatalism. "An event is necessary," means simply that it can be determined, and "to determine" means to describe with precision. All determinations are made on the supposition of the presence of certain conditions and the absence of any other factors which might interfere.

the right-angled triangle, which is the distance between sun and earth. In this way human reason bridges over the gap between the known and the unknown.

Reality possesses certain features which can be determined, not by experience, but *a priori*, by purely formal thought, i. e., by pure reason.

There is this peculiarity about our reasoning, that the first act determines the following acts. When we construct an equilateral triangle, we cannot help also making the angles equal; and when we construct an equiangular triangle, we cannot help making the sides equal. This is a puzzling fact to those who look upon the world as a sum of many incoherent items. It is all but inexplicable from the nominalistic standpoint. But it is only a more complex case of the fact, that when we have determined A to be A, we cannot at the same time determine it to be *not A*. By positing A, A is A and remains *A in all its consequences*. Only by inverting reason itself, can I say that A is A and *not A* at the same time.

What is reason?

We present as a preliminary definition the statement that reason is man's method of thinking. Noiré says: "Man thinks because he speaks"; and Max Müller, standing upon the same ground, adds: "No language without reason, no reason without language." We are quite willing to adopt the results of modern philology, but they are not sufficient for our present purpose. Our problem is deeper still. We accept the Noiré-Müller theory and may restate it as follows: Language is the organ of rational thought, and rational thought develops through the mechanism of language. Our present problem, however, is not How did human reason develop? but How is it possible that our reason can give us information about reality?

Not all processes of reasoning give us information about reality, but only such as are carried on with consistency. Thus we have to modify our preliminary definition of reason. Reason is not any process of reasoning, but a certain and quite definite kind of reasoning, and reasoning is rational only when it agrees with this one kind of reasoning. Accordingly we define reason as "the norm of reasoning."

We ask, Is there any norm of reasoning? In this form the question again reminds us of the old problem of realism *versus* nominalism. Is there any universality, generality, or necessity? Our answer is affirmative.

One thing is pre-eminently characteristic of reason, viz. that there is but one reason. There are not various reasons. Reason (if it is reason at all) is the same in one man as in another man. As there is but one kind of arithmetic, so there is but one kind of reason.

Reason in the sense of "norm of reasoning" is to be used without the article. If a man gives *a* reason for his action, or if he speaks of *the* reason he has, he means the rational motives or principles by which he allows himself to be influenced. Such reasons are various and of different natures; but reason as the norm of reasoning, is no individual or particular thing or idea; its very nature is generality or rather universality. And it is a real feature of existence.

Mathematicians with great ingenuity have invented various kinds of mathematics. They have shown that Euclidean geometry is but one actual case among many possible instances. Space might be curved, it might be more than three-dimensional. But no one has yet been bold enough to propound a theory of curved reason.

And why should there not as well exist a curved logic as a mathematics of curved space? A curved logic would be a very original innovation for which no patent has yet been applied for. What a splendid opportunity to acquire Riemann's fame in the domain of logic!

We must let this fine opportunity of propounding a new and extremely original conception of reason slip away, for we are not in a disposition to make good use of it. A curved reason would be simply crooked reason, for the rigid sameness of reason prevents us admitting any different kinds of reason.

The inmost nature of reason is consistency, and thus the simplest statement of rational thought is the maxim of sameness formulated in logic in the sentence $A = A$. The formula $A = A$ is, as it were, the straight line of logic; but with this difference that we can imagine as possible (although not as actual) the straight lines of curved spaces, but not a logic that abandons what might be called "the axiom of consistency."

The axiom of parallels in geometry corresponds to the syllogism in logic. Inconsistent reason, a reason which does not acknowledge the truth expressed in the formula $A=A$, which can accept the existence and non-existence of a thing at the same time is pseudo-reason; and if pseudo-reason as a possible case by the side of actual reason were a legitimate assumption, all thinking would cease and all being would be thrown into confusion, reason would be nonsense and the world a chaos, everything would be a medley without coherence, without rhyme or reason, a vast bedlam, and reason itself would present an exceptional case, unaccountable, odd, strange, exceptional, brought about perhaps incidentally as a happy chance. But how this reason could be of any objective use would present new difficulties. For reason being only an incidental chance occurrence in our brain would have no applicability to the objects around us. Of a triangle which we constructed in our mind, we could, perhaps, from three known parts, determine the other unknown parts. But it would be impossible for this mental model of a triangle to give us information about a real triangle formed by the sun, the moon, and the earth. And when information thus acquired was found to be correct, we should be confronted with an all but miraculous coincidence.

There are two classes of formal sciences, the one is characterised by geometry, the other by logic, algebra, and arithmetic. The former we have on another occasion called purely formal, the other rigidly formal, the rigidly formal being a special kind of the purely formal. The rigidly formal sciences are products of our mental operations. There is no assumption, no hypothesis, no knowledge of the actual forms of the world in it. The other formal sciences, such as Euclidean geometry, assumes that space is of a certain nature. Space is a pure form of the world; but that space is such as it is, we know through experience. We cannot by pure reason alone prove that space is tri-dimensional or that it is homaloidal.

Reason is not merely purely formal, it is rigidly formal. Reason is unequivocally determined; and when we say "all men are mortal and Caius is a man," we can by no means escape the conclusion that Caius is mortal.

The rigidly formal being in its applications strictly reliable in experience, there is no other explanation than to think of experience as possessed of the same nature as our thought. There is an analogy between mental operations and natural processes which proves that they are ultimately of the same kind.

When we consider the events of the world in their simplest possible conditions, we resolve it into innumerable processes of motion, as a constant shifting about. There are separations and combinations, and wherever the same separations and combinations take place there are also the same results. This sameness, which can be formulated as a law, viz., that the same produces the same, is a reality, and indeed the most real reality, for it lies at the bottom of the cosmic nature of the world; it implies that existence is not a chaotic chance medley, but a cosmos permeated by uniformities and regulated by laws. All laws will in the end have to be recognised as mere corollaries of this simplest of all laws, which is nothing but the self-consistency of being. This fundamental law is by its very nature eternal and universal; it thus constitutes an intrinsic and inalienable quality of existence; and no existence can be without it. To be sure, it is a purely formal law, for it tells us nothing as to the substance, the material, the sensations, or other qualities of being; but for that reason it is not less real. The formal, indeed, is the most important part of reality, for the forms of things make the things in their individuality what they are.

The same operations which are active everywhere, separations and combinations, build up the human frame, and in the human frame also man's mind. Human reason is a structure built up by mind operations; and pure reason is a mental construction of them in abstract purity. The human mind being a part of the world, we find that the law of sameness holds good also for the products of purely mental operations: the same operations yield the same results. Moreover, there will be an agreement of the constructions of pure reason and the laws that obtain in them with the configurations of reality and the purely formal laws of the universe. This agreement was the puzzle of Kant, which led him astray into the by-paths of his transcendental idealism; and yet this agreement is nothing but the law of sameness, which he neither doubted as a logical law, nor as a feature of reality. He might, with the same reason, be puzzled because one egg looks like another.

Experience, viz., the effect of events upon sentient beings, is caused by sense-impressions and consists of sensations. Every sensation is a feeling of a certain kind and form, and the various sensations are interrelated. Thus we have (1) the properly feeling element, or the sentient or sensory part of a sensation, and (2) its formal or relational aspect.

When we consider *in abstracto* these two qualities, the purely formal on the one hand and the purely sensory on the other, we are struck by a peculiar contrast. We attribute necessity and universality to the formal, while the phenomena of the sensory exhibit such an irregularity that we can never attain to the certainty that they are the same in one case as in another.

No amount of sense-experience, be it ever so large, can justify the proposition, that "because something has been so in nine hundred and ninety-nine cases it will also be the same in the thousandth case." While, contrariwise, one case of experience of a formal consideration, for instance, that the equality of sides in a triangle constitutes an equality of the angles at its base is sufficient to establish a universal rule.

This contrast has given many a headache to Mr. Mill and his followers, but they have never solved the problem; nor can they solve it so long as they cling to the principle from which the sensational school starts, that all knowledge is and remains a mere association of single sensations; a principle which overlooks the important contrast between the formal and the material. Says Mr. Mill in his System of Logic, III, chap. iii, § 3 :

"There are cases in which we reckon with the most unfailing confidence upon uniformity, and other cases in which we do not count upon it at all. In some we feel complete assurance that the future will resemble the past, the unknown be precisely similar to the known. In others, however invariable may be the result obtained from the instances which have been observed, we draw from them no more than a very feeble presumption that the like result will hold in all other cases. That a straight line is the shortest distance between two points, we do not doubt to be true even in the region of the fixed stars.

"Why is a single instance, in some cases, sufficient for a complete induction, while in others, myriads of concurring instances, without a single exception known or presumed, go such a very little way toward establishing a universal proposition? Whoever can answer this question knows more of the philosophy of logic than the wisest of the ancients, and has solved the problem of induction."

He who does not see the contrast between the formal and the material, between that which imparts necessity to conclusions and the incidental features of experience, between the universal and the particular, can never arrive at scientific certainty, and he will naturally be puzzled at his own boldness when he unhesitatingly accepts some conclusion, based perhaps upon one single observation, as of universal application.

The formal sciences are systematic; they are produced by construction and can thus exhaust all possibilities of a case, while our sensory experience bears the character of the incidental; all information through the senses is only in parts. And why is that so?

We perform certain operations, for instance, in arithmetic we add and subtract, and we invest the products of our operations with certain symbols. We call $1+1$ "two" (denoted by the sign "2") and $1+1+1$ "three" (denoted by the sign "3"); and we find that the product of the operation $1+1$ is the same as the product of the operation $3-1$, viz., $=2$. This is so and will be so whenever we repeat the operation; and this quality that it will always be so is called "necessity" or "rigidity."

The whole mystery of logical necessity consists in this, that exactly the same operation will always bring about exactly the same product. The same is true of all purely formal operations. Unforeseen interferences of unknown powers being excluded from this domain of abstraction, we can pronounce with absolute certainty the verdict that in this sense twice two will under all circumstances be four.

The objection has been made that twice two may be five in other worlds, but we reject this view as absurd. We willingly grant that two bacilli plus two bacilli might be five or even five hundred and more bacilli, because they might rapidly multiply during the operation. This is quite possible in the tube of the microscopist, but it is impossible in mathematics, for in the realm of abstract thought all such possibilities are excluded. There we measure or count only our mental operations. When counting our mental steps only, we cannot have made five hundred steps when we have made only four.

Having constructed in our mind systems of formal thought, such as numbers, geometrical figures, the logical categories, etc., we are in possession of schedules which serve us for reference when dealing with the real world, and their infallible rigidity is extremely useful in extending the sphere of our knowledge.

Having constructed by certain mental operations (which in their elementary forms are very simple indeed, being upon the whole nothing but a combining, separating, and recombining) we possess in the products of our formal thought an instrument that enables us to deal with single experiences and to systematise them into exact, scientific, and philosophical knowledge ; in other words, we possess reason.

Reason originates by a differentiation of the formal and the sensory in experience. As soon as the formal has been separated in thought from the sensory, as soon as an animal learns to speak, to count, and to think in abstracts, it has developed reason. Reason does not rise out of the sensory element of our sensations and memory-images, but out of their interrelations. Reason is the product of abstract thought-operations, and pure reason is a system of empty forms whose office it is to arrange in good order and to systematise further experience.

Reason is not an arbitrary invention, it is not the product of a hap-hazard association: reason is the method of our experience and the norm of all thinking.

Experience is the natural revelation of existence to sentient beings; reality impresses itself upon their sentiency and thus forms their notions. But we find that all the impressions of experience possess in spite of their infinite variety certain features in common, and these universal features develop in the course of the mental evolution of sentient beings into those notions which in their systematic unity are called "reason."

Reason is not purely subjective. Reason is objective in its nature. Our subjective reason, human reason, or the rationality of our mind grows out of that world-order which we may call the rationality of existence. Human reason is only the reflection of the world-reason, the former is rational only in so far as it agrees with the latter.

Reason (i. e. human reason) in its elementary beginnings consists first of the operations that take place among mental images. Mental operations are the germ of reason, and mental operations are as such the same as any other operations, the same as any process that takes place in nature. Reason is, secondly, a mental picture of certain qualities of reality; and being the picture of a universal feature of reality, it conveys information applicable to all reality. Thus reason is, thirdly, an instrument which enables us methodically and critically to deal with any kind of experience.

ABSTRACTION.

The importance of understanding the process and scope of abstraction is very great, for abstraction is the very essence and nature of man's method of thought. The ability of thinking in abstracts distinguishes him from the rest of the animal world, for abstraction is the main function of reason, and abstract thought is almost a synonym of rational thought.

Abstraction is a very simple process, and yet some of the greatest philosophers have misunderstood it. He, however, who is not clear on this subject, or neglects the rules of abstraction, will never be able to attain accuracy or lucidity of thought.

The greatest difficulty for a child when he learns to walk is, not to stumble over his own feet. Similarly, the greatest difficulty with philosophers is, not to stumble over their own ideas. All our ideas are abstractions, and different abstractions represent different qualities of the objects which we meet in experience. In order to preserve clearness of thought, we must not confound the different ideas, and must not transfer a certain abstract that belongs to one set of abstractions into another quite different domain of abstractions. At the same time, we must never leave out of sight that the reality from which our abstractions are made is one inseparable unity.

The very existence of many problems proves how little the nature of abstract ideas is understood. There is, for instance, the question which has again and again been raised, whether the soul can be explained from matter or energy. The question itself is wrong, and proves that the questioner stumbles over his own ideas. We might just as well ask whether matter can be explained from energy, or energy from matter. Matter and energy are two different kinds of abstraction, and feelings, or states of consciousness, are again another kind. We cannot explain an idea by confounding it with other heterogeneous ideas. What should we say, for instance, of a man who spoke of blue or green ideas, or who attempted an explanation of mathematical problems from the law of gravitation? What should we say of a philosopher who sought to determine whether ideas could be explained from the ink in which they are written?

Our abstracts are stored away, as it were, in different drawers and boxes. Any one who expects to solve problems that confound two sets of abstractions, has either stored his ideas improperly or searches for them in the wrong box.

If a problem is hopelessly entangled, we cannot solve it, and being led to regard the confusion of our mind as a true image of the world : we come to the conclusion that the world is incomprehensible; that is, we fall into agnosticism. But such is the confusion generally prevailing, that the man who reaches the conclusion that all things are at bottom utterly unknowable, becomes the leading philosopher of the time. Mr. Spencer actually declares in his famous work, "The Data of Psychology," that "the substance of mind" (sic !) is unknowable.

Mr. Spencer searches for his explanation of mind in the wrong box.

Misunderstand the nature of abstraction and an impenetrable mist will cover all your thinking and philosophising.

Says Professor Huxley in an address on Descartes's "Discourse":

"If I say that *impenetrability* is a property of matter, all that I can really mean is that the consciousness I call *extension* and the consciousness I call *resistance*, constantly accompany one another. Why and how they are thus related is a mystery."

He first abstracts two qualities, viz., extension and resistance, from one and the same thing, and then wonders why they are constantly found together. Besides, unless we identify the two ideas, extension and resistance are not always joined together. The surrounding air is extended, but does not perceptibly resist, unless confined so that it cannot escape. Extension and resistance, of course, always accompany one another if, as in physics, extension is used as a synonym of resistance, if extending means exercising a pressure or resisting. Where is the mystery that fluidity is always accompanied by liquidity, that inflammability is always found together with ignitability, etc.?

Professor Huxley has stored ideas which belong in the same box in different boxes.

* * *

Some philosophers forget very easily that our ideas are not reality itself, but representations of reality. They are symbols, representing certain features of reality. While our ideas of different spheres partly overlap, partly exclude each other, reality itself, from which they have been abstracted, is not a "combination" of heterogeneous existences. On the contrary, we must always bear in mind that the totality of the world is an inseparable unity. All reality is one great whole, and our ideas draw limits between the different provinces that are of a purely ideal nature.

Ideas, and especially abstract ideas, are symbols that serve for orientation in the world. They help us to find our bearings. Energy is not matter, and matter is not energy, but for that very reason there is no matter without energy, or energy without matter. In the same way consciousness is neither matter nor energy, but consciousness for that reason is not a thing in itself. It is not an independent existence that exists apart from matter or energy. Things in themselves, in the sense of separate and independent entities, do not exist. But philosophers are too apt to regard their abstract ideas (their noumena) as representing things in themselves. Thus time is not space, and space is not time, and neither the one nor the other is material; but we are not therefore justified in conceiving of time or space as things in themselves. In brief, all abstracts represent features of that great inseparable whole which is called reality, the world, the universe, or nature. Matter is not an inscrutable entity, but a name for that quality which all material things have in common. Space and time are thought-constructions built of abstract notions representing certain relations of things. And the inside world of man, the states of his consciousness, his sensations, perceptions, and ideas, no less than all other abstracts, form one special sphere of abstraction—the domain of psychology.

*　*　*

The words *abstract* and *abstraction* are derived from the Late Latin *abstractum* and *abstractio*, the latter being the act of abstracting, the former the product of abstraction. The old Romans did not use the words *abstractio* and *abstractum* in a philosophical sense. These ideas are a product of the great nominalistic controversy and first appear in the twelfth century. Abstraction was originally used in contrast to "subtraction." Abstraction was the consideration of form apart from matter, and subtraction the consideration of the essence without heeding its form.*

Modern usage has dropped the scholastic distinction between "abstract" and "subtract" entirely, and places the abstract in opposition either to the "concrete" or to the "intuitional," i. e. the direct perception of objects.

Abstraction means "to single out, to separate and hold in thought."

For instance: when observing the whiteness of snow, we concentrate our attention upon the quality of whiteness, to the neglect of all the rest. Attention, accordingly, is the condition of abstraction. Special wants produce special interests; special interests produce special attention, and a special attention singles out and keeps in mind that which is wanted.

Abstraction is first a concentration of attention, involving the neglect of everything else, then a mental separation of the part or quality upon which the attention is concentrated, and finally the establishment of a relative independence of the product of abstraction. This completes the function of abstraction, and as this can be done only by naming, abstract thought is identical with rational thought, which is the characteristic feature of the thought of speaking beings.

This is the reason why abstract thought is upon earth the exclusive prerogative of man; and why brutes are incapable of abstract thought. The process

---

* See *Century Dictionary*, s. v. abstract.

of naming is the mechanism of abstraction, for names establish the mental independence of the objects named.

As soon as the color of the snow has been denoted, the word designating snowish color or whiteness becomes applicable as a thought-symbol to the same quality wherever it is found.

* * *

The verb, "to abstract," is used, according to Drobisch, either in a logical or psychological sense; in the former we abstract certain qualities *of* a given complex, in the latter we abstract our attention *from* certain objects. (See Mansel, "Prolegomena Logica," 3d ed., p. 30.) Hamilton regards the former usage as improper. Says Hamilton:

"I noticed the improper use of the term 'abstraction' by many philosophers, in applying it to that on which the attention is converged. This we may indeed be said to prescind, but not to abstract. Thus, let A, B, C be three qualities of an object. We prescind A, in *abstracting from* B and C, but we cannot without impropriety say that we abstract A."

In agreement with Hamilton, Sully remarks:

"Abstraction means etymologically the active withdrawal of attention from one thing in order to fix it on another thing."

The Century Dictionary adds to this quotation:

"This is all founded on a false notion of the origin of the term."

The old quarrels between Nominalists and Realists, important though they were, are forgotten. The distinction between "abstract" and "subtract" has lost its meaning. Hamilton and Sully's usages have not been accepted outside some narrow circles of English scholars ; and the most natural and common usage of the verb "to abstract," it seems to us, is in the sense "to form abstracts," or "to make an abstraction." We abstract a certain quality of a certain thing, (say whiteness) and treat it in our thought as if it were a thing itself.

* * *

Intuition, in the proper sense of the term, i. e. *Anschauung* or atsight, furnishes the immediate data of our sense-impressions. (See p. 9 et seqq. of this book.) Man's thought, i. e., the properly human of his mind-operations, consists in an analysis and reconstruction of his *Anschauungen*, intuitions, or atsights, i. e., of the data given him in his sense-impressions. With the assistance of language, man separates and recombines certain features of his atsights ; he constructs ideas, which enable him to find out in the events of nature the determining factors and to make them, on a large scale, subservient to his wants.

Man's ideas, and most so his general ideas or generalisations, in so far as they are represented by names, are products of abstract thought. The idea "horse" is not the actual and concrete reality of the sight of an individual horse, but a generalisation ; it is a name representing to every English-speaking man the composite image of all horses, or pictures of horses seen, and including, in addition, all the knowledge he has of horses. The general idea of a horse thus stands in contrast to real horses; it is not the horse itself, but a thought-symbol signifying horse in general.

Abstract thought is decried as pale, colorless, shadowy, and unreal. True enough, in a certain sense, for abstract thought is not intuition, it is not *Anschauung*, and therefore it cannot possess the vivid glow of sensuous activity, the reality, individuality, directness, and immediateness of the objects presented to our senses. Yet, in another sense, abstract ideas are not at all unreal.

The atsights of our sense-experience are the basis of all abstract ideas. The atsights are the real facts, our abstract ideas, however, are artifices invented for the purpose of better dealing with facts; they are reality-describing symbols and well-designed mental tools.

* * *

The term "abstract" is confined to such products of thought-operations as "whiteness, goodness, virtue, courage," etc.; but it is sometimes also employed to denote generalisations such as "star," meaning any kind of a star, or "triangle," meaning any kind of a triangle. The fact is that generalisations can be made only by the method of abstraction. The term "abstract" is not used, however, to denote sensations. Sensations are the materials which by abstraction are analysed into their elements, for sensations are that which is given in our intuition, i. e. our *Anschauung*, and abstracts are contrasted to the intuitional.

This is very well, and we do not blame this usage of the word; but we wish to point out that even sensations are in their way a kind of abstraction. Our sense-organs perform the function of abstracting certain features of the objects impressing us. Thus the eye abstracts only certain ether-vibrations called light, and transforms them into vision, the ear abstracts only air-vibrations and transforms them into sounds, the muscular sense abstracts resistance and transforms it into the notion of corporeality, the skin abstracts temperature and transforms it into sensations of heat and cold. The tongue and the nose actually abstract and bodily absorb certain particles, and transform the awareness of this process into taste and smell.

Thus it is evident that abstraction is a function of fundamental application in the domain of psychic life, and the method of abstraction is, properly considered, not limited to that sphere which, according to the generally accepted terminology, is called the domain of abstraction.

THE ABSOLUTE.

Of all abstract ideas, none, perhaps, has played a more important part in philosophical thought than the term "absolute."

The mischief which the term "absolute" has caused in almost all antiquated philosophies is hardly conceivable. It actually plays the part of a fetish among a certain class of sages, who, as soon as their thinking capacity, either from innate inability or from natural laziness, ceases to accomplish its purpose, request their readers and adherents to bow down into the dust and worship the Absolute.

The absolute is an idol which is still worshipped and which must be broken to make room for a purer, clearer, and truer conception of philosophy.

We present the following definitions of the term absolute*: (1) That which is not related. (2) That which is not conditioned. (3) That which is entire, complete, or perfect. (4) That which is viewed without regard to its relations or conditions as a complete whole.

The term "absolute" is used in contradistinction to "relative." That which is not relative is absolute. The most important relations being those which condition the existence of a thing, the term came to be identical with the unconditioned or that which has the conditions of being in itself. This raised the dignity of the word above all its comrades and it became a substitute for God, for God alone can be described as "unconditioned." Those philosophers, accordingly, who have ceased to believe in God, but have not outgrown the paganism of antediluvian religions, find it very convenient to enthrone a divinity of their own

* The word is derived from the Latin *absolutum*, meaning that which has been loosened from.

make, and to treat it with the same awe and reverence that marks the behavior of fetish worshippers.

Let us review the philosophical meanings of the term. Absolute is used in the sense of "that which is not related." Very well! Such a thing as "that which is not related" does not exist. The world is a system of relations and there is nothing that is or can be unrelated. Even the God of Genesis (i. e. according to the traditional notion) is not an absolute being. He stands in a definite relation to the world as its creator, ruler, and master. The God of the New Testament being He in whom we live and move and have our being can still less be called absolute; and the Universe as such, the All, the totality of being (whether we include God as a part of it or regard the Universe with materialists or atheists simply as a big lump of material atoms) is as little absolute as either a supernatural or an immanent God, for the All has certain relations to its parts. In a word, the absolute in the first sense is simply a humbug.

The "absolute" in the second sense, as that which is not conditioned, is, perhaps, admissible, although it would be an improper expression for that which ought to be called the unconditioned. For the "unconditioned" or "that which has the conditions of its being in itself" is not a concrete thing, a special being, or a big person inside or outside of the world, but a certain feature existing in all the realities to be met with in experience. All things, all creatures, all concrete realities or beings, as such, are forms; they originate by being shaped, they disappear by being dissolved, but there is a certain something in them which abides in all the changes, and this certain something is part and parcel of their existence.

Here is not the place to discuss what this feature of an abiding something in all the various forms of being is. It most certainly is not only matter and energy as the materialists say, it is also that within of nature which in its highest evolution appears as consciousness; mainly that peculiarity of the formal laws which establishes harmony and makes them so axiom-like, "self-evident," as they have been called, that through them the whole universe becomes transparent like glass to the eyes of the initiated. In all these abiding features of fleeting existences there obtains an inalienable consistency of being with itself which gives to the world the character of *Gesetzmässigkeit*, so that uniformities prevail which can be formulated in so-called "natural laws," so that the totality of the world is not a chaos but a cosmos, a whole in which order prevails.

Something "unconditioned" in this sense exists in the abiding features of the various existences. But it is obvious that this something that abides is not absolute; it is not without relations to the other more or less fleeting forms of realities. Moreover, we cannot so much say that it is unconditioned as that it conditions the very existence of every thing that is.

The absolute in the third sense is identical with the All, including everything and anything, past, present, and future, also all the chances of its possible formations. The All alone is a perfect entirety, a complete whole in itself, which has no relations to things outside, because there are none, the All including everything.

This conception of "absolute" is quite legitimate, but the expression "All" being free from the mystical tinge that still adheres to the term "absolute" is preferable. We can only use the term absolute in this sense as an *epitheton ornans* for the All in All, not as its name; yet as an *epitheton ornans* it has little significance.

The "absolute" in the fourth sense expresses, not a quality of or in things, but a certain attitude of the thinking subject. In this sense, it has a loose and rather popular application. Thus we speak of the "absolute certainty" of mathematics, meaning thereby simply its universal reliability*; there may be special cases, but there are no exceptions to mathematical theorems. We speak of "absolute monarchy," looking at monarchy abstractly and meaning thereby that according to the law of the country the monarch is not bound to give account to any one for the acts of his rule or misrule. We speak of "absolute (i. e., the highest imaginable) perfection," of "absolute (i. e., perfect) beauty," "absolute (i. e., pure) alcohol," "ab-

---

* Mathematical axioms possess absolute certainty in the sense mentioned above; they are reliable statements. But they are not absolute truths, i. e., truths which need not be proved.

solute zero" of temperature, which is —459.4°. All these terms and many more similar phrases are sanctioned by usage, but nowhere is there any real absoluteness as a quality of things; there is only a relative absoluteness, a lack of relations in some special directions or a perfection or finish of some kind.

Thus the usage of the term "absolute" in these and similar connections is not to be understood in any strict or philosophical sense of the word, but is a license quite allowable for special purposes.

It would lead us too far here to refer to all the nonsense that has been written by philosophers who declare that "philosophy is ultimately, by its very nature, a search for the Absolute" (with a capital A).

No greater absurdity has been excogitated by a great man than the idea of things in themselves, which really means "things absolute." (See *The Monist*, Vol. II, No. 2, "Are There Things in Themselves?") Hegel's system has been characterised as the philosophy of the absolute. He maintains, as Flemming sums up his doctrine, that "all existence is strictly a manifestation of the Absolute in the evolution of Being, according to dialectic." The truth is that all existence is existence, and the idea of absolute existence is nothing but a pale thought, an abstract symbol created by dialectic to represent those qualities which all existences possess in common. To represent the absolute, this shadow of being, as real, and existence as a mere manifestation of it, is turning the universe topsyturvy.

NOUMENA AND REALITY.

The main mistake of the early philosophers was their habit of regarding abstracts as independent real entities, or essences. The pagans represented beauty as a goddess and worshipped it, and Plato thought that ideas were beings that possess an independent existence outside and above the sphere of reality, of that reality which is faced by us and depicted in our sensations.

Abstracts are thoughts and Kant called them *Gedankenwesen* (things of thought) or *noumena** which he contrasted with *Sinneswesen* (things of sense) or *phenomena*. The latter, a synonym of *Anschauungen* or atsights, are the data of experience, the former are the theories derived therefrom.

Their abstract nature being recognised, we have ceased to regard noumena as metaphysical essences or mysterious beings. They are no longer substantiated. In fact, just the contrary has happened. The pendulum has swung from the one extreme to the other, and it is now customary, to regard abstract ideas in contradiction to the old view as mere fictions and nonentities. One error is naturally followed by the opposite error. But abstracts are not mere fictions, they are

---

* Noumenon, literally translated, means "thought" and not as the dictionaries almost *unisono* have it (the Century Dictionary among them) "anything perceived." It is derived from νοεῖν "to think," not "to perceive." Νοῦς means "understanding" and not "perception" or "sense." The correct pronunciation is "nŏ-oo'menon" and not "noomenon."

symbols *representing features of real existence,* and *as such* they cannot be overestimated, for they form the properly human in man, they create his dignity and give him the power he possesses.

Even our systems of mathematics, arithmetic, and other sciences of pure thought are not mere fictions or arbitrary inventions, but constructions made of elements representing actual features of reality, of pure forms and of the relations of pure forms. To be sure, they are fictions in a certain sense; they are inventions, but they are not mere fictions and not arbitrary inventions. To operate with pure forms, as if pure forms as such existed, is a fiction. But exactly in the same way it is a fiction to speak of whiteness as if whiteness in itself existed. The processes of addition, subtraction, multiplication, division, involution, evolution, the usage of logarithms are inventions, but they are as little arbitrary inventions as, for instance, the method of naming things. All these inventions (like other useful inventions) have been called forth by special wants; most of them have been eagerly searched for, and they serve certain practical purposes.

*   *   *

Noumena represent certain features of, or relations among, phenomena. Ideas are symbols of reality. Abstract thoughts are comparable to bills or checks in the money market. Bills and checks are not real values themselves, but, being orders to pay out a certain amount, they represent real values, thus serving to facilitate and economise the exchange of goods. In the same way the realities of life are the data of experience as they appear in our *Anschauung*; abstract ideas, however, are derived from and have reference to these basic facts of our existence. Although the values of our abstract ideas are ultimately founded upon the reality of the given facts of experience, bearing to them the relation that bills or drafts bear to gold bullion or cash money;[1] no one who is a capitalist in the domain of knowledge, can do without them, for he needs them for the utilisation and practical control of his wealth. But it is comparatively easy to palm off counterfeit abstracts at their nominal value upon ignorant or uncritical people who know not the difference; for the poor fellows who have thus been cheated are likely to die before they discover the fraud.

Goethe says in one of his distichs:[2]

"Fürsten prägen so oft auf kaum versilbertes Kupfer
  Ihr bedeutendes Bild; lange betrügt sich das Volk.
Schwärmer prägen den Stempel des Geists auf Lügen und Unsinn.
  Wem der Probierstein fehlt, hält sie für redliches Gold."

Princes are coining mean coppers that poorly are plated with silver,
  Stamping their portraits thereon. Long the deceit remains hid.
Thus the enthusiast stampeth, as genuine, nonsense and errors.
  Many accept them as good, lacking the touchstone of truth.

---

[1] Cf. page 1, last paragraph.

[2] *Goethe and Schiller's Xenions.* Selected and translated by Paul Carus. Chicago: The Open Court Publishing Co. 1896.

Most people being uncritical, we need not wonder that the philosophical world is flooded with abstracts that possess no merit beyond being high-sounding words. There are plenty of philosophical wild-cat banks flourishing and booming, and this is quite natural, for our average public is no better than the savages of darkest Africa with whom glass pearls pass for money, the same as if they were genuine.

THE PROBLEMS OF EXPERIENCE SOLVABLE BY THE METHODS OF PHILOSOPHY.

CAUSATION.

CAUSE AND EFFECT.

THE problem of causation is a test-question, the solution of which is highly characteristic and of fundamental importance. If you wish to know a thinker and the nature of his philosophy, ask him what he understands by "cause." Both the statement and the solution of many other philosophical and ethical problems depend on the answer given to this question.

What is a cause?

A cause is that which produces an effect.

The terms *cause* and *effect* belong together; they are correlates. There are no causes without effects, there are no effects without causes.

What is an effect?

An effect is a state of things produced by some event, action, or process.

Everything we see has a special form or is in a special place; it is somehow and somewhat; it is in a special condition or state. Yet whatever its nature or substance be, its form, or mode of being, its suchness, is the result of events. These events which form and mould things are called their "causes."

We distinguish causes and circumstances; causes being events which by their *motion* produce effects, and circumstances being conditions which, though always *at rest* or at least relatively at rest when the cause happens, yet exercise, directly or indirectly, a determinative influence upon the result.

If there be several factors that produce by coöperation an effect, we can either speak of several causes, or may, according to the special purpose of our investigation, denote only the most important one as the cause, counting the others as circumstances.

This conception of cause is plain enough. We say, for instance, the touch of a key on the piano is the cause of any of the succeeding events contingent thereon, viz., of the motion of the hammer in the piano, of the vibration of the chord, or of the sound perceived by the ear.

CAUSE AND REASON.

There is another sense, however, in which the term cause is frequently used. By cause is often understood that quality of things by which their peculiar action is explained. Thus gravity is said to be the "cause" of the falling of a stone. The elasticity of the vibrating chord is said to be the "cause" of the notes which it emits.

This kind of cause is identical with what from another point of view is called the forces of nature.

Now, we are at perfect liberty to give the name cause either to the *events* which produce effects or to the so-called *forces of nature* by which we explain phenomena; but we should not give the same name to both; they are things of too different a nature to be classed in one and the same category. The latter, being the explanations by which we account for the efficiency of causes, are better called "reasons"; and so we propose to distinguish between "causes" and "reasons." Unless we distinguish causes and reasons we are apt to fall into confusion.

Let us consider the two ideas "cause" and "reason," that the distinction may be clear.

Causes are always special and concrete events; single facts; certain definite happenings, which occur or have occurred in a certain place and at a certain time. Reasons are general ideas expressing qualities of things; they are universal rules concerning the nature of such qualities; they are natural laws applicable wherever and whenever things are possessed of these qualities.

Thus, the cause of the stone's fall is the particular event that pushed the stone over the edge of the precipice. The cause may have been the movement of a man, who shoved the stone till it started to roll; other determining circumstances being the precipice, the mass of our planet, its atmospheric resistance, etc. But the reason why the stone fell is the reason why stones *generally* fall, and why *all* masses gravitate.

When we ask the reason why a certain thing acts in a special way, or why a certain event takes place under certain circumstances, we expect as an answer a description of the qualities of the things under consideration. Now, the reasons of natural phenomena are formulated in natural laws. Qualities are the causative in the cause; they are that which makes things move or act in a special way, and natural laws are general formulas that describe the qualities of things.

The reason of the stone's fall is, that the stone possesses a certain quality called gravity which makes the stone gravitate toward the centre of the earth. The action of gravity is constant; it is a force present in the stone; it is an inseparable property of its mass, and its action has been formulated in a natural law called the law of gravity or gravitation.

REASON AND CONSEQUENCE.

The correlative term of cause is effect, that of reason is consequence. The Germans interrelate *Ursache* and *Wirkung* on the one hand and *Grund* and *Folge* on the other. A man who speaks of the effects of a reason or of the consequences of a cause forms word-combinations that have no sense. We say "consequence," not "sequence." Consequence conveys quite a different idea from sequence. Consequence is logical, sequence is temporal.

The (logical) consequence of a reason is that which it implies, or involves. The statement All men are mortal, implies that Socrates is mortal. Mortality is a mark of *all* men; this is the reason why such single men as Socrates are also to be declared mortal. Thus the consequence is not a sequence, not a temporal succession, for it is necessarily coëxistent with its reason. The effect is a temporal sequence; the consequence, on the other hand, is a logical conclusion; it points out to us what is involved in the reason. The equal-sidedness of a triangle involves by implication that it is also equal-angled. If a dog is a mammal, he is also an animal. Neither the one nor the other quality is temporally prior, both are temporally simultaneous: the term consequence signifies a *mental* succession, a ὕστερον πρὸς ἡμᾶς.

A DISTINCTION NEEDED.

If we were to call "causes" and "reasons" by one and the same name, what a bewildering confusion would arise! If we called both "causes," some causes would be the antecedents of their effects. This all real causes are. Other causes, however, would be simultaneous with their effects. This all reasons are. The gravity of a stone, for instance, persists. The stone still gravitates toward the centre of the earth after it has fallen. Thus, the cause would exist even after its effect.

Says the Latin proverb: *Cessante causa cessat effectus.* This is nonsensical, for every cause is ended when its effect has appeared. The touch of a key on the piano represents a certain expenditure of energy which is transferred, first to the hammer, and then to the chord, which at once begins to vibrate. These vibrations are then transferred to the air, and through the air to the acoustic nerve and to the brain, where the vibrations are felt as a peculiar sensation. There is a constant transfer of energy taking place, and the cause is always past as soon as the effect appears, for, though the cause continues to exist in the effect, it ceases to exist in its original form; every effect is its cause transformed under special circumstances.

The Latin proverb should read: *Cessante ratione cessat consequens.* If a certain reason ceases, its consequence also will cease. For reasons are simultaneous with their consequences.

Take the following facts as an example:

The mercury in the barometer does not flow out at the open end, because the atmosphere exercises a certain pressure on it. The atmospheric pressure is a certain quality of things, which, so long as it lasts, obtains with all its consequences. The fluctuations of the pressure are accompanied with a rise or a fall of the barometer, and if they ceased altogether, or almost altogether, as, for instance, under the air-pump, the mercury would flow out. Thus the barometer can be used as an indicator of air-pressure. The consequence of a certain reason is employed as a means of information.

The difference between "cause" and "reason" is marked in all languages. The logical spirit of the speech of the various nations is wiser than our philosophers.

The Greeks distinguish between $αἰτία$ (cause) and $ἀρχή$ (principle, beginning, reason), the Romans between *causa* and *ratio*, the French and all other Romance nations between *cause* and *raison d'être*, the Germans between *Ursache* and *Grund*. Popular usage is, as a rule, very accurate; but those who should be the leaders of the thought of the people have become blind guides of the blind, who lead them astray. The people use these words correctly; those who are chiefly to be blamed for their misuse are our professional thinkers.

ARISTOTLE ON CAUSATION.

What confusion reigns in the four meanings in which Aristotle (as handed down to us in his books) proposes to use the term "cause"! He distinguishes (1) the formal cause, or $τὸ\ τί\ ἦν\ εἶναι$, that which makes the thing such as it is; (2) the material cause, or $ἡ\ ὕλη\ καὶ\ τὸ\ ὑποκείμενον$, saying that the brass of a statue is its cause; (3) the start of the motion, or ὅθεν ἡ ἀρχὴ τῆς κινήσεως [this alone is a real cause]; and (4) the end in view, or τὸ οὗ ἕνεκα, the "wherefore."

We are tempted to believe that we have before us in Aristotle's works, not the master's own exposition, but the bungling notes of a superficial disciple; for there is no system in the doctrine of the four causes. Aristotle's distinctions, as they stand, have no sense. But sense might easily be introduced into them by slightly altering the report.

Aristotle might have said that we must note in causation: (1) the material; (2) the formal; (3) the cause; and (4) the effect. These four things are not four kinds of causes, but are four points to be minded in all causation. The first and second points are two aspects demanding consideration; but neither substance nor form are causes, causation being the transformation of substance. The third point is the cause, viz., the motion through which the transformation takes place, while the fourth one is the end attained, the effect, or purpose, i. e. the effect desired.

If the agent is a living and thinking being, so that the whence of the motion (τὸ ὅθεν τῆς κινήσεως) is a motor-idea, the effect, or the whither of causation, is pursued with consciousness, and the effect aimed at is called purpose, or the end of the cause.

There would be rhyme and reason in Aristotle's four points, if he had treated them in the manner briefly sketched here; but as the various passages in which the subject is treated actually stand, they appear as the loose talk of a rambling mind. The author of the Aristotelian books as they now read (most likely not Aristotle himself, but one of his auditors) apparrently repeats his recollections of an ill-digested lecture and fills out the gaps of his incomplete notes with his own misconceptions.

CONFUSED NOTIONS OF CAUSATION.

It would repay one's trouble to go over the entire field of philosophical literature and collate the mistakes made by prominent philosophers in the conception of causation, for the harvest would be very great. Thus Lucretius says:

"Felix qui potuit rerum cognoscere causas."

[Happy the man who could comprehend the causes of objects.]

Yet Lucretius means: "Happy the man who could understand the *reasons* of all things."

* * *

Spinoza speaks of *causa sui* and means *ratio sui*. A *causa sui*, a cause which is the cause of itself, is sheer nonsense, while *ratio sui* is at least not nonsensical. A *ratio sui* is a reason which requires no further explanation; it denotes some quality of existence which is universal, so that we need not look for a more general one under which it can be subsumed. In this sense *ratio sui* is equivalent to *ultimate reason*.

It has been said that "science is a search for causes and philosophy for the causes of causes." The meaning of this saying is that science is a search for reasons and philosophy for ultimate reasons. We want to know why things act in a special way, or, in other words, we want to become acquainted with the qualities of which things are possessed.

* * *

The pious expression "First Cause" is also only a misnomer for "ultimate reason." If, supposing we knew all reasons, we continually ascended from one reason to another, we should at last arrive at an ultimate reason, which is that reason from which all other reasons can be deduced, and all the reasons together would form one great system. This "ultimate reason" is sometimes wrongly supposed to be capable of affording us a key to all the problems of the universe. It is thought to be a kind of centre from which all the parts are quickened with the reason of their being, and is then identified with God.

This is the metaphysical conception of God. The philosopher fills an empty, abstract idea with mysteries and worships the errors of his own brain.

We must not forget that the ultimate reason (even if we had it quite clear in our mind) does not and cannot, of itself alone, explain the rest of the world. The more general our ideas become, the emptier they are. It is true that general ideas serve as explanations for less general ideas, but they provide us only with one part of the explanation; the other part has to be added by the particular conditions to which they are applied. The universe does not possess somewhere a secret nook from which we can understand the whole in the sense "Faust" imagines when he says:

> "*Dass ich erkenne, was die Welt*
> *Im Innersten zusammenhält.*"

And similarly the God of the universe is neither in a particular place, as a great world-ego, nor does he reside in any special ideal centre, such as a general notion. God is concrete and real, being everywhere that element which makes things be. To mankind the idea of God has never been either the mythological conception of theologians or the abstract cloud of philosophers; the idea of God in practical life may not have been thought out clearly in the minds of the people, but it has always been that something in existence which demands obedience; it was always the authority of conduct, which we have to mind and to which we have to adapt ourselves; it was always a moral idea.

God should never be identified with so grotesque an idea as a "first cause"; and to pray to the "First Cause" is about on the same level as to pray to the "Ultimate Effect."

* * *

Schopenhauer has written a whole monograph on Causation; yet so little does he distinguish between cause and reason that he calls every cause "a sufficient reason" and entitles his book, "Ueber die vierfache Wurzel des Satzes vom zureichenden Grunde" (On the four-fold root of the principle of sufficient reason). He speaks of *Erkenntnissgrund, Seinsgrund, Reiz, Motiv,* and *Ursache,* as if all were causes and reasons at the same time.* The various kinds of causes, such as stimuli and motives, are, of course, not comparable to roots, but are rather branches of causation.

* * *

Reid claims that "causation is not an object of sense." So far he is right, for our notion of causation is not a product of sensation, but of reflection. Our ideas of cause and effect are noumena; they are results of thought, not phenomena, not sense-perceptions. But Reid is wrong when he claims that causation "is to be admitted as a first or self-evident principle." ("Intellectual Powers," Essay VI, Chap. VI.) There are no such things as self-evident principles. If we limit (with Kant) the term "experience" to sense-experience, we must agree with Reid that "experience is surely too narrow a foundation" for it. But if we include in experience our rational reflection upon the events which form the objects of our observation, we should say that our notion of causation is safely and firmly based upon experience.

---

* One of Schopenhauer's four roots, so-called, is not a cause, but a reason, viz., the third one, which he calls *Erkenntnissgrund.*

George Henry Lewes says in one place ("Probl.," First Series, Vol. II, p. 323):

"Cause is the group of conditions which pass into the effect, ideally distinguishable from the product, but not really separable."

And again (First Series, Vol. I, p. 330):

"Causation is immanent change."

This is cause in the commonly accepted sense; it is cause as we understand the term. Yet his investigations lead him to identify not only Cause and Law, but even Cause, Law, and Fact. He says (First Series, Vol. I, p. 336):

"Had the essential identity of Law, Cause, and Fact been duly apprehended, much misty speculation would have been dissipated."

Facts are single and concrete events, while laws are abstract descriptions of qualities of facts that are of a general nature. This is a radical difference! How can causes be identified with both facts *and* laws? Causes (viz., causes in the sense in which we use the term) are facts, but laws are "reasons."

Locke defines cause as

"A substance exerting its power into act to make one thing to begin to be."

And in a similar way Lewes says (First Series, Vol. II, p. 350):

"A glass of punch is made by adding together whiskey, water, sugar, and lemon; each of these elements we know separately, and know them as the cause of the punch."

This kind of cause, in the language of traditional Aristotelianism, is called "the material cause"; but the term is very misleading. A cause is never a substance, or a thing, or an object, or a material body. A cause is always a motion, an event, or a happening of some kind. The cause of the punch is the act of mixing its ingredients; but the materials of which it consists are no causes. Otherwise, we ought to call oxygen, hydrogen, nitrogen, etc., the causes of man, because human tissues consist of these materials; paper and printer's ink would be the causes of books; iron and wood the causes of machinery.

* * *

If causes were material things, what cause could be offered for events, which, as such, are not material. What is, for instance, the cause of a death?

The famous instance invented to show that cause and effect are quite disparate and cannot be brought into an equation by which to demonstrate their identity, according to the scholastic theorem *causa æquat effectum*, proposes "mercury" as "the cause of death."

Says Mr. Lewes (First Series, Vol. II, pp. 337, 338):

"The mercury or antecedent is said to be the cause, the paralysis, or consequent, the effect. Could any two things or events be more unlike? Can we say that the cause, mercury, has among its properties the peculiar property of paralysis? We cannot, for we know that paralysis is a condition of the organism, not of the metal; and it is only in this special conjunction of these two agents—metal and organism—that the result appears."

Mr. Lewes is quite right, that "the result appears in this special conjunction"; he adds:

"The effect will be the completed process, and the efficient causes are the factors in that process."

Yet he should have added that the main mistake is to call "mercury" a cause. Not the thing mercury is the cause of death, but "the administration of mercury," which under given circumstances produces such transformations in the organism that its vital actions cease altogether—a state which we call death.

Says Mr. Lewes (First Series, Vol. II, p. 346):

"Every event that happens has a cause, everything that exists is a cause. This is evident."

The truth is exactly the reverse. We must say, "Everything that exists has a cause," which means that everything as it is at present possesses its form and nature so as to be what it is by antecedent conditions which formed it. Everything is the result of causes and circumstances. And we must further say: "Everything that happens is a cause"; that is to say, every event which produces a change is a factor in the transformation of a special field of existence; every event is an agent in the causation of certain effects resulting therefrom.

The misconception of causes as "objects which follow one another" led Hume to regard succession as the main characteristic feature of causation. He could discover no necessary connection between antecedents and their sequences, and thus he became a sceptic. Truly, there is no necessary connection between arsenic or mercury and death. There is no similarity between cannon-balls or shells and a desolate citadel. And even if there were a necessary connection or similarity or identity among objects that are wrongly called causes and effects, it would avail nothing, for "objects" assuredly are not interrelated as causes and effects.

* * *

The theorem *causa æquat effectum* is wrong. The cause is never equal to its effect. What remains equal in the act of causation is simply the total amount of matter and energy; that which does not remain the same is the form; and the difference of form is all-important. The difference of form constitutes the new state of things called the effect, and if the effect were not different from its cause, there would be no change, and we should not be entitled to speak of causation at all.

CAUSATION NOT MERE SUCCESSION.

The idea of regarding causation as a mere sucession of antecedents and sequences misses the essential nature of causation, for it leaves out of view the fact that causation is a transformation of a definite amount of matter and energy, without any increase or decrease of substance. When omitting this, the most essential feature of causation, we can, of course, find no connection between two such things as mercury and death, and the whole process becomes mystical, with the result that we have no choice left but to surrender all hope of ever unravelling the problem. Yet we have, in that case, artificially raised the dust which prevents us from seeing. We have ourselves produced the confusion by confounding the issues, and have therefore no right to say that causation is an inscrutable mystery, because we have made a muddle of it.

The statement that we can observe only antecedents and sequences, but can discover no necessary connection among them, appears very guarded, yet it is, after all, a mere misstatement of the case. For indeed we can observe transformations, and all transformations are successions of events which possess a very obvious connection.

To discuss causes and effects without even mentioning that they are phases in processes of transformation, is something like writing a book on mechanics without speaking of motions, or acting Hamlet with the rôle of Hamlet omitted.

EXPLANATION AND COMPREHENSION.

The business of science consists, first, in observation; second, in explanation; and third, in application.

First we have to observe a process, that is, we have to describe the whole event, to search for the motion which starts it, and also to take note of the action of the circumstances. The process as a whole constitutes what we call a system of transformation.

Having made many observations of similar and of diverse kinds, we proceed to explain them : that is, we make them plain ; we describe them in such a way that the determining factors of the transformation are placed in relief and the indifferent circumstances dropped.

Explanation is systematic description. An explanation is complete when we can so trace all changes that all the details of a process are recognised as transformations.

Being in possession of an explanation we can practically apply it to future experience by adjusting the course of events so that favorable conditions may be obtained and dangers avoided.

Our desire for explanation is not satisfied with a formulation of the qualities of things as they are in single cases. We want reasons which will apply to all cases of the kind. Again, every law of nature which describes the action of things in a general formula, applicable to all actions of the same kind, calls for further explanation. We want reasons for our reasons. We want to know how two laws, which apparently are very different because describing the actions of reality in different conditions, are, after all, two applications only of one and the same fundamental law. Our need of explanation impels us to rise from special laws to more general laws, until all are comprehended in universal laws. Now, this method of subsuming a number of instances under one common point of view is called "comprehension." Comprehension is a higher kind of explanation. Thus, all knowledge describing the qualities of things would form one great system of laws; and if we were omniscient we should see at a glance how one and the same law operates in all other laws.

Laws being descriptions of reality, an omniscient being would intuitively see that reality is the same everywhere, and that its fundamental quality remains what it is throughout; it is only differentiated according to conditions and in the innumerable variations which we meet with in experience.

CAUSATION AS TRANSFORMATION.

The law of causation is a law of motion; it describes a transformation that takes place, and as in a transformation the form only is changed, causation means substantially the same thing as the conservation of matter and energy. When we observe a process in which the effect can be shown to be the product of a transformation, our desire for explanation is satisfied. But we are always sore perplexed when we are confronted with something that is not the product of a transformation. We should be nonplussed if we were ever to observe the creation of matter or energy out of nothing, or, *vice versa*, witness an instance of the annihilation of either the one or the other. We see, thus that the world is explainable wherever its events are exhibited as transformations.

So far as science has gone, it has met with many problems that defy explanation, but nowhere has it discovered an instance in which a thing could be proved not to be a case of transformation. The faith of science in the reliability of the law of causation has never been shattered.

TELEOLOGY.

The problem of causation involves another problem which may be called the problem of teleology.

Aristotle, we have seen, mentions besides "efficient causes" also "final causes," and the history of philosophy is replete with quarrels as to the admissibility of final causes. There are some philosophers who admit the existence only of efficient causes, while there are others who claim that there exist both efficient causes and final causes. The latter understand by "final causes" what is commonly called "purposes," "ends in view," "aims," or "plans of action."

A little reflection will teach us that there is but one kind of causes, and that this one kind of causes is, at the same time, always efficient and final. If a cause is not "efficient" it is no cause, and if it is not "final" or, in other words, if it leads to no result, to no end, it can have no effect, and a cause without an effect is no cause. What would causation be if either its cause or its effects were cut off?

Thus, all causes being efficient, to speak of "efficient" causes is gratuitous; and to speak of "final" causes is misleading. The term "final cause" is a word-combination which has just as little and just as much sense as the term "causal effect." As every cause is final, so every effect is causal.

Every transformation is a motion and every motion pursues a definite direction; it has a whence and a whither. The whence is called the cause, the whither the effect; the whence is the beginning of the process, the whither its end.

This is true both of the stone that falls to the ground and of the stone that is thrown with purposive intention. Every motion has a direction, an aim, which is conditioned by the tendencies inherent in the moving bodies. The aim may not be reached. Thus, the aim of the falling stone is the centre of the earth; the aim of a thrown stone may be a window. The falling stone never reaches the centre of the earth, and the bad boy who tries to break a window-pane may miss his aim. But the tendencies to reach the aims are, nevertheless, factors in the process of causation; they are not always realised, perhaps, because of other factors which curtail their efficiency.

The aim or goal (the tendency) of a motion is called purpose when it is pursued with consciousness.

The falling stone has a definite tendency, in accord with the nature of its gravity, but it has no purpose. Thinking beings alone can have purposes.

That the aims of the actions of inanimate things must show a certain regularity, an orderliness, or harmony, if but the qualities of the things upon which their tendencies are contingent remain the same, is obvious. Thus we can readily understand that the stellar universe, in agreement with mechanical laws, arranges its masses in a harmonious order so as to produce milky ways and solar systems. We can see how certain chemical substances will assume certain regular shapes, the form of which depends upon their angle of crystallisation. We can further understand how the functions of organised substances will differentiate so as to form the organs of organisms. In one word, the harmony of nature appears as an immanent, intrinsic, and necessary teleology.

The term teleology, *Zweckmässigkeit*, or finality, i. e., a harmony of the effects of causation, has been wrongly used to denote conscious design, and the problem has been viewed as if there were a dilemma between purposive design or plan on the one side, and pure chance or haphazard accident on the other. The truth is, that we find in the realm of inanimate nature neither consciously devised calculations of certain effects, nor purely accidental results of blind chance, but an irrefragable order presenting a regularity of action according to the constancy of the qualities of things. The nature of the universe continuing to be the same, the laws of its being remaining immutable, and its substance enduring in matter as well as in energy, it follows of necessity that the course of events exhibits throughout regularities and uniformities. However, those who deny teleology, are not less mistaken than their opponents. A world of which all events are factors of causation is necessarily a teleological world—a world of law, an orderly arranged universe, a cosmos with definite tendencies which determine the direction of the evolution of its life-phenomena.

FREE-WILL.

There are so many superstitions connected with the word *cause* that one sometimes feels tempted to discard it altogether. And we should indeed advocate the abandonment of the term if it were not difficult to replace it. If we discarded it, a new term must be invented to denote the truth contained in the word.

After all, it seems to be easier to purify old terms than to replace them by new ones. New terms are more liable to be misunderstood than the criticism of old terms. Criticism, if sound and generally acceptable, will serve as a sufficient corrective.

The idea cause is often looked upon with awe and reverence, as if it were an independent and sovereign being, and thus the necessity of causation is regarded as a power which rules the world with an iron rod.

We have learned that all effects in the process of causation are strictly determined by their causes and circumstances. Causation implies necessity; and necessity means that every event is determined by its conditions in its minutest details.

Does not this doctrine abolish free-will? It almost seems so, but a close investigation of the problem will show that it does not. Necessity is by no means contradictory to free-will. Both ideas are compatible.

What do we understand by freedom?

When a man can act as he pleases, we call him free; but when he is under restraint, when he cannot follow the motives which stir him, when he is compelled by others to act against his will, he is not free.

The actions of a free man are the immediate expressions of his character. If we wish to know the character of a man, we must observe how he acts when at perfect liberty. The actions of a man that is not free, are not the expressions of his character; they manifest some other power which curtails his liberty. But every man, whether free or unfree, will act under given circumstances in such a way that, if his character and all the circumstances are known, his action can be determined; it can be described as it will happen.

The confusion from which so many errors arise is due to the similarity of the ideas "compulsion" and "necessity." Compulsion and necessity are not always synonyms. Compulsion annihilates free-will. Necessity is the inevitable consequence by which a certain result follows according to a certain reason.

Freedom, in the sense we conceive it, is not limited to the domain of man's activity. Nature is not a dead machine which is set in motion by push and pressure. Nature is throughout possessed of a living spontaneity, and the spontaneity of nature appears in the action of things according to their qualities. The actions of things exhibit the nature of things.

We can classify all phenomena as primary and secondary motions. Primary motions arise from the nature of things; while secondary motions are transfers of primary motion through push and pressure. Primary motions are spontaneous, and the freedom of nature appears in their display. Secondary motions, sometimes called purely mechanical phenomena, originating through the impacts of spontaneous motions, are comparable to compulsion in the domain of psychology. They are actions in which the nature of the agent, i. e., of the body in motion, is not revealed; they show the influence of some power foreign to the moving thing. The motion of the horse is spontaneous, but the motion of the cart drawn by the horse is purely mechanical.*

The attempt has been made again and again to explain natural phenomena mechanically, as due to some kind of pressure. This method is founded on a

* The word "spontaneous" is derived from the Latin *spons* (will). We call those actions "spontaneous" which rise from the will, the character, the nature of things. See *The Monist*, Vol. III, No. 1, p. 91.

confusion of thought. To say that "all motions take place according to mechanical laws, viz., the laws of motion," is quite a different proposition from maintaining that "everything can be explained by mechanical laws." We can explain all motions by mechanical laws, provided the masses and the moving forces are given, but we cannot explain the existence of the moving forces themselves by mechanical laws.

The futility of a mechanical explanation of the world is apparent as soon as we understand that purely mechanical phenomena cannot have risen from themselves. They are due to the spontaneous motions of nature. And a mechanical explanation of the spontaneity of nature hitches the cart before the horse. How can the secondary motions produce primary motions? We might as well explain the motion of the horse as due to the pressure of the cart behind him.

We regard the existence of primary motions in nature as an undeniable fact. The ultimate springs of reality are spontaneous forces, and their manifestations are a true exhibit of the nature of being. The spontaneity of nature is analogous to the action of a free will.

Give the magnet freedom on a pivot and it will turn toward the north, in accordance with the qualities of its magnetism. If you direct the magnet by a pressure of the finger to some other point, you will exercise a compulsion that will prevent it from exhibiting its real nature. Were the magnet endowed with sentiment and gifted with the power of speech, it would say in the first case, "I am free, and of my free will I point toward the north." In the second case, however, it would feel that it is acted upon and forced into some other direction against its nature; it is possessed of a tendency to resist the pressure; it rebels against it, but is not strong enough to overcome it, and would declare its freedom curtailed.

The moral worth of a man depends entirely upon what motives direct his will. An estimate of moral actions is possible only on the condition that they are an expression of his free will. The best action would amount to nothing if it were a mere chance result which might have been otherwise. The chief value of moral deeds rests on the fact that the man who performed them, could not, under the conditions, act otherwise; that it was an act of free-will, and, at the same time, according to his character, of inevitable necessity.

FATALISM AND NECESSITARIANISM.

We distinguish between necessitarianism and fatalism. Necessitarianism is the doctrine that everything is determined by its conditions; while fatalism means that no matter what a man may do, his fate is predetermined.

While necessitarianism is a sound doctrine and a theory without which science would be impossible, fatalism is a superstition.

Those who look upon necessity as a power residing outside of or above nature will naturally make no distinction between necessitarianism and fatalism ; nor will they understand that necessity does not exclude free will.

The ancients believed in a deity called Moira, which was supposed to have power even over the immortal gods. Necessity, however, is not the Moira of Greek paganism, nor the Fate of the Romans, nor the Kismet of the Mohammedans. Necessity is not the compulsion of natural events. Necessity is the inevitable determinedness of events by the nature of the things in action.

When we say that the falling stone obeys the laws of gravitation, we introduce a dualistic world-conception into our statement. The law of gravitation is not the power which compels the stone to fall ; it is a formula which describes in a comprehensive way the action of gravitating bodies. The gravity which makes a stone fall is an intrinsic quality of the stone. The stone, while falling, is not obedient to any law outside of it, but acts according to its nature. The action of the stone is spontaneous, and he who is acquainted with the nature of the stone can, according to the circumstances, determine its action.

All events in this world are determined ; some of them are determined by the nature of the moving things, while others are due to compulsion. Nature possesses a certain character, and this character is revealed in its spontaneous actions.

The fatalistic view of the world conceives nature and man alike as dead mechanisms, acted upon and subject to a power which is not in themselves. Necessitarianism, as we have defined it, is monistic. It shows that nature is no mere display of mechanical forces, but full of independence, life, and spontaneity, the highest efflorescence of which appears in the freedom of man.

THE CHARACTER OF NATURE.

All the actions of a man, diverse as they may be, will be of a certain type, because his character is the ground from which they start; and his character remaining to a certain extent the same throughout his life, all he does, says, and intends, will, within reasonable limits contingent upon the changes of his character, be in unfailing harmony. His virtues and his vices will bear some resemblance. They will correspond with one another and show their common origin.

In the same way chemical materials will show under certain circumstances certain qualities. Phosphorus shines in the dark; it is inflammable; it melts at a temperature of so many degrees; such and such is its specific gravity, etc. And all these properties form single characteristics of this element which we call phosphorus. In order to find out the nature of things, we must put them to different tests, called experiments, so as to find out how they operate under different circumstances. The nature of things appears in their tendencies to act, and their actions are a revelation of their qualities.

The character of man and the properties of things are inquired into in the same way, according to the law of causation. And whosoever would get at the truth of what the nature of the universe may be, must observe its actions and search for the ends and aims to which its development tends. In this way alone can we understand the character of existence, for the development of natural events in their entirety is the revelation of the cosmos.

When we have to deal with a man, we must know his character. When the chemist operates with drugs he must know their properties; and he who wants to adapt himself to the world in which he lives must know the character of nature.

* * *

The light which the theory of evolution throws upon our knowledge of nature shows that the development of the world is constantly tending toward a higher plane and a better arrangement. The amount of matter, as we learn from the law of the conservation of matter, remains unchanged, but the form and composition of matter is changeable. The arrangement in which the elements are combined may be more or less favorable, and this arrangement undergoes a constant alteration according to the law of cause and effect.

In the realm of organised life there is a tendency to advancement observable, the aim of which is the improvement of the present state. But the improvement is only possible by unceasing struggle and heroic work; not in the service of egotism, but in that of a higher unity, conceived as higher than the existence of the individual; not by indulging in the happiness of the present, but by severe labor done in the hope of and with a faith in a better future; in a word, it is only possible by sacrifice.

The world-constitution is such that it implies duties, and the attendance to the duties of life consists in a constant struggle for advancement, progress, and amelioration; and the world-conception which recognises this state of things is called "Meliorism."

The struggle for advancement and the aspirations of moral endeavor in general are not a matter of individual choice, so that we may or may not acknowledge the authority of its ideals. They are an inevitable presence in the world and no living creature can withdraw itself from their influence. They constitute an authority for conduct which is not dependent upon our likes or dislikes and cannot be disregarded with impunity.

Every individual has to sacrifice his youth's best years for the comfort of his age, and in like manner humanity sacrifices the labor and the lives of its individuals for a better future. On the road of perpetual sacrifice the human race throngs onward to a higher and better existence; and should races similar to humanity on earth live on other planets, we may be fully convinced that on those planets also there is an evolution taking place to higher states of existence.

The way by which life advances and the means through which it attains this end is called morality.

All living existences possess tendencies to form higher unities. Like organs which operate as parts of an organism, they work, they suffer, they sacrifice themselves for the good of the whole of which they are members.

Let us look at the lowest forms of life. Cells possess in general all the properties of organic beings; alimentation, growth, and propagation. A mother cell having divided itself, is still connected with its filial cells; and several cells are in their union more fit to encounter the struggle for life. Henceforth, the work to be done for their preservation is divided in such a way that some cells perform one, other cells another, function for the unity thus created. It is a division of labor according to a general plan, and that is what constitutes an organism. The single organ or limb of a body does not exist of itself, but is subservient to the larger unity of which it feels itself a part. The purpose, aim, and end of its existence is no longer in itself but in something higher than itself. This principle pervades all organised nature. Organisms cannot exist but under this condition, and this principle is ethical.

The same principle that produced organisms and animals, guides them in their future development. And only so far as a creature is animated by this ethical guidance is it able to develop into something higher. This principle is the star of Bethlehem that leads the leaders of the human races to the cradle where a new truth is born, or where the germ of a higher development is thriving. Thus the existence of man, of his bodily organism, and the society of the man as a social organism, rest on the same principle. We find everywhere an aspiration to develop to a higher unity and a better existence.

The next higher stage to which development ever tends is the ideal, and there will be no rest in the minds of men until the ideal is realised. After that, new ideals arise and lead on in the interminable, infinite path of progress not merely ruled, as Darwin says, by the famous law of the struggle for life, but enhanced by the strife for the ideal.

The ideal is no mere fiction. It is a power of reality pervading the universe as the law of nature, and in humanity's case it points out to man the path of progress. Progress, if it is guided by the ideal, will produce new and better eras for human kind, and if a moral tendency were not the fundamental law of nature, there could not be any advancement, development, or evolution.

Nature and the laws of nature are sometimes complained of as immoral, but such a conception of nature has no sense. It is based upon an anthropomorphic view of nature. Nature is neither moral nor immoral, but unmoral. Nature's creatures only are moral or immoral, according as they do, or do not, conform to the laws of nature.

That power in nature which under penalty of destruction enforces a certain conduct is called by the religious name "God." God is the authority of conduct, and the name "God" signifies a reality as much as any natural law. Obedience to God is morality, disobedience, immorality.

Those who claim that God, or nature, or both, are immoral, have either a wrong conception of morality or an insufficient knowledge of the nature of things and the laws of evolution.

The nature of morality cannot be established by *a priori* reasoning, but by experience and a scientific investigation of the data of experience. Scientific investigation tends more and more plainly to show that the morality of our traditional religions is, upon the whole, correct. The moral rules propounded by the great religious teachers of mankind prove an instinctive but deep insight into the order of nature. That which according to their precedent we are in the habit of calling morality can be demonstrated to agree with the constitution of the universe.

In this sense, to live naturally becomes identical

with aspiring morally. We are all parts of a whole greater than ourselves, and our very being is intimately connected with our surroundings, viz., with the fates of our fellow-men, with the remotest past, and also with the most distant future.

The innate qualities and talents which appear as gifts of nature, are, according to the theory of evolution, faculties or combinations of faculties, inherited from ancestors. The labor of former generations is not lost. Its fruit has been preserved and handed down to the generation now living. This fact has a profoundly ethical import. There is nothing without work in this world. The easy and apparently effortless production which we admire in genius is only possible by inherited abilities, acquired by the labor of ancestors. Every man ought to be conscious of the fact that he is the product of the labor of ages, and whatever he does, be it evil or good, will live after him so far as his individuality impresses itself and influences his contemporaries. In consideration of this fact, man will think of the past with reverence and work out his future with earnestness.

The aspirations to ever higher aims on the highroad of eternity seems to be the inmost, the sublimest, and the grandest of nature's tendencies. And although the solar system in which we live should, after its due time, fall to pieces, there are other suns with their planets developing, in which, no doubt, the same principle is as active as it is in this world of ours.

Sursum is the watchword of all evolution, and the aim everywhere perceptible. The means by which it is attained is morality. The source from which this tendency starts is the wonderful spring that marvellously and mysteriously quickens all the parts of the universe.

PSYCHOLOGY.

THE ASSOCIATION PHILOSOPHY.

"Association" (from the Latin *ad*, "to," and *socius*, "an ally") originally denotes the act of becoming, or the state of being, a confederate, and is generally used in the sense of a connection of persons, things, or ideas.

The association of ideas plays an important part in psychology. Ideas which are related possess the quality of involuntarily calling one another into consciousness. Our mind is full of associations, and our brain is filled with commissural fibres which may fairly be regarded as the paths of association.

Psychologists have taken much pains to formulate the laws of association, and have come to the conclusion that there are different kinds of associations, among which must be mentioned those by contiguity, similarity, and contrast.

If two impressions have been made simultaneously, the one will recall the other. This is called the association of contiguity, and this contiguity may be one of time or one of space: it may be simultaneity, or it may be a coincidence of events in one and the same place, or both.

Again, suppose a child has seen an elephant for the first time in a menagerie, and now sees another in a street-parade; he will think of the first elephant and also of the surroundings in which he saw him. The present image of the street-parade elephant becomes associated with and awakens the memory-image of the menagerie elephant. This is association by similarity. At the same time it calls to mind other impressions incidentally associated by contiguity.

Now imagine a philosopher, who has devoted his life to a study of the schoolmen and their quarrels. As soon as he hears the word "nominalist," he thinks of their opponents, the "realists." These names are closely connected in his brain, and this connection is called association by contrast.

The explanation of these facts appears simple enough. Two impressions are made at the same time, and it is natural that their traces should be as closely connected as were their original ideas. Moreover, that ideas will revive the memory-images to which they bear a strong resemblance is easily explained by the theory that nervous actions of a peculiar form will naturally travel in the paths of their own form; they follow the lines prepared for them by former actions of the same kind.

The fact that ideas are actually associated with each other, together with the obvious simplicity with which this fact can be explained, has induced a great number of psychologists to believe that the theory of association affords a key to all the problems of the soul. The psychology of association is represented by Hobbes, Hume, Hartley, the two Mills, Herbert Spencer, Höffding, and others, and it may be said to be in full bloom to-day.

The association of ideas is a very important factor in soul-life, but it does not explain the problems that have caused the greatest difficulties to our philosophers. The association of ideas does not explain the origin of concepts, of generalisations, of abstracts; it does not explain the origin of reason; it does not explain the origin of the idea of necessary connection which we attribute to certain relations.

The association philosophy is an error, because it applies one special thing (the association of ideas) to the whole realm of psychical life, and thus makes of it a fundamental principle in philosophy. The association philosopher resolves all the more complex psychical facts into associations of single sense-impressions; he regards the idea of causation as a mere association of a frequently repeated sequence; thus making reason a mere incidental and purely subjective habit of association, and depriving it of stringent authority, objectivity, and necessity.

Let us first consider the psychological mistakes of the association philosophy. Generic images do not originate by association, but by fusion. Many images are superimposed like composite photographs and form a composite image, in which all the common features are strongly marked, while the incongruent features appear blurred. The association of ideas is quite another and, indeed, a very different process from the blending of images. The former preserves the single pictures distinct, the latter welds all particular impressions into a higher and more general unity.

He who fails to distinguish these two processes, association and fusion, and tries to conceive of a generic image as the product of association, will be perplexed in many ways; and, indeed, almost all the attempts that have been made to explain association by similarity from that by contiguity, or *vice versa*, bear evidence of the sad confusion that prevails among the association philosophers. Some of them despair of reducing the various associations to unity, and either ask us to look upon it as an evidence of dualism or declare that the mystery is too deep for our comprehension.

The process of causation has, in the conception of the association philosophy, ceased to be a necessary event and has become a mere sequence, which is at best an invariable sequence. Thus the bond of union that holds the world together as one inseparable whole is lost, and all events become isolated particulars, single happenings without any intrinsic or necessary interconnection. The universe, which to us is a systematic and consistent cosmos, is, from the standpoint of the association philosophy, comparable to a bag of innumerable peas; many events happen to follow the one upon the other, but there is no true necessity, no real causation, no intrinsic order or harmony.

The association philosophy rests upon the principle that all knowledge is derived from experience. So far, good! But the association philosophers, having inherited all the errors of sensationalism, take the idea "experience" in the limited sense of the word. In the spirit of nominalism, of which they are an offshoot, they see isolated phenomena only and are not aware of the bond of union which permeates the whole realm of existence, giving rise to the uniformities that science formulates into natural laws. The possibility of formulating a law of nature, appears, from their standpoint, an insoluble mystery.

The association philosophy fails to satisfy the demands that must be made of a philosophy. It leaves the most important problems unexplained, and by its assumptions and hypotheses involves us in such hopeless intricacies that we must ultimately take refuge either in scepticism, agnosticism, or mysticism; and something must be wrong in a system of explanations, a philosophy, or a science, which comes to the conclusion that we cannot explain things, that they are unknowable or utterly mysterious.

The association philosophy forms a contrast to Kant's apriorism. The philosophy which we propose avoids on the one hand, the fallacies of Kantian apriorism, and on the other those of the association philosophy. Our view does not end in agnosticism or mysticism, but affords a satisfactory explanation of why we attribute to the formal sciences necessity and universality. It explains how mind originates, how general ideas are formed, how knowledge (and not only mere opinion) is possible, and teaches us the usage of the proper methods of scientific inquiry.

COMPOSITES OF BLENDED MEMORIES.

To procure truly representative faces, Mr. Francis Galton invented the method of composite portraiture; he photographed whole classes of persons, one after another, upon the same photographer's plate, so adjusting and superimposing the different faces that all eyes fell in the same horizontal, and all noses in the same vertical line. The results which he obtained are remarkable. They "bring into evidence all the traits in which there is agreement, and leave but a ghost of a trace of individual peculiarities. There are so many traits in common of all faces that the composite picture when made from many compounds is far from being a blur; it has altogether the look of an ideal composition."

Now, suppose that the photographer's sensitive plate were endowed with actual sentiency. We should have in that case a state of things similar to what actually exists in the brains of living beings. Similar impressions are made through the different sense-organs and registered in their respective sensory centres.

Registrations of the same kind are not made side by side; they are not independent single pictures; they are placed one upon another and blend, all forming a peculiar new formation, viz., a composite memory-structure or an ideal image of all the objects of the same kind that have come under observation. To express it in two words, they are not associations, but fusions.

When a special sense-impression is made, the nervous disturbance travels on the path prepared by former sense-impressions of the same kind to the interior structures of the hemispheres containing their traces as a composite memory-picture. The present sense-impression, being felt to be the same in kind as the old ones registered in its analogous composite, naturally serves as an indicator of the presence of an object of the same kind as those that caused the former sense-impressions. Thus sense-impressions become signs of things, and the composite memory-images acquire meaning. These meaning-endowed sentient composites constitute the elements of the soul.

THE NATURE OF PERCEPTIONS.

Perhaps everybody has sometime in his experience been puzzled at the sight of an object the character of which he was unable to recognise. We see a certain something and do not know what it is. The outlines perhaps are clear, the colors distinct; but, nevertheless, we cannot make out what kind of a thing it is.

What can this psychical phenomenon teach us?

It teaches that a sense-impression is quite a different thing from a perception. A sense-impression that is felt is called a "sensation." But a perception is more. A sensation may be perfect yet a perception need not be effected. A perception is effected only when the sense-impression is transmitted to the memory-structures of its class so that it is *interpreted* as a certain object, is identified with former impressions of the same kind, and clearly recognised as such and such a thing.

That which has been called the cerebral centre of vision, is nothing but the place in which the composite memories of sight-impressions are stored. A creature whose centre of vision has been destroyed has lost the repository of those impressions which it has received through the eye. It is soul-blind, or *seelen-blind*, as it has been called by German savants. Again, that which has been called the centre of hearing is nothing but the place in which composite memories of auditory impressions are contained; and a creature whose centre of hearing has been destroyed can no longer recognise sounds. It is soul-deaf, or *seelen-taub*. And the same is true of all the so-called centres of soul-life.

Professor Goltz has succeeded in keeping alive a dog whose entire hemispheres had been removed. While all other organs, especially his senses, are in perfect order, he has lost all his memory-structures, and with them the composite images shaped by his former experiences. Thus he is a perfect idiot, a soulless creature, capable of receiving sense-impressions through all his sensory-organs, but unable to interpret their meaning.

A perception is the simplest act of cognition, for a perception is a sensation that has reached and revived its analogous memory-structure. There, so to say, it is subsumed. Having the same or a similar form, the sense-impression fits into the form of the memory-structures and is felt to be of the same kind. This classification of things of the same kind is the essential nature of cognition : perceptions are primitive judgments.

GENERALISATION PRIOR TO COGNITION.

There has been much controversy concerning the priority of general or of particular ideas. It was declared, on the one hand, that general ideas had sprung from particular ideas: the *primum appellatum* and *primum cognitum*, it was maintained, were concrete objects. While on the other hand, it was objected that the very first act of naming, and indeed every act of cognition, presupposes the existence of a general idea. The latter view is quite correct; yet, when this view is adduced to prove the mysteriousness of cognition, implying that there is a break in nature between man and the rest of nature (as proposed by Prof. F. Max Müller in *The Monist*, I., 4), we must seriously protest.

If we keep before our minds the physiological process of perception, the reason is obvious why every idea must at bottom be a general idea, and why every act of cognition presupposes some general notion under which a particular notion is subsumed. Every sense-impression is a particular fact, while the analogous memory-structure, which is ready to receive any sense-impression of the same kind, is, or at least stands for, a general notion. And this notion is the more vague, the more primitive it is.

Generalisation, accordingly, is not one of the highest faculties of the mind, but the very lowest. Mind begins with generalisation.

The first sensation is a particular act; it is no notion. But the first memory-trace of a composite partakes of the nature of a generalisation; when revived by a later sensation, it represents a whole class, and therefore the first perception, i. e., the first and most rudimentary act of cognition is a subsumption; it presupposes already the existence of a general notion.

APPERCEPTION AND CONSCIOUSNESS.

A perception is, in turn, the most elementary act of apperception; and apperception is the function of consciousness.

In analysing the nature of consciousness, we find that it consists of coördinating, centralising, and intensifying feelings in a focus. A single and isolated feeling cannot exist as an actual feeling. It becomes an actual feeling only when it meets another feeling by which it is felt. Thus feelings are possible only in those organisms in which feelings are so organised or systematised that sensations are referred to the memories of former sense-impressions, and this is accomplished by the nervous system.

Suppose a sense-impression is made upon a sentient organism void of memories—i. e., on an organism which has never as yet received prior sense-impressions. The isolated feeling produced by such a first sense-impression (if feeling it can be called) is very different from later feelings, for its scale of consciousness is not merely extremely low, but actually zero, there being no other feeling to apperceive it. The second sense-impression of the same kind, however, meets with and revives the trace left by the first one. It is received in the memory-structure of the first sense-impression and there it is felt. This act of the memory-structure is the weakest kind of apperception imaginable; it is the first tiny appearance of consciousness.

Isolated feelings may be called feelings, but they are not felt. Several or at least two feelings must meet to be felt.

The stronger and the more manifold the memory-structures grow, the more cognisant does apperception become. A sense-impression will in higher stages revive several memory structures, and their feelings will be concentrated upon it. The object of attention is now focussed, and the act of its being felt is intensified by a coördination of feelings. Thus dim feelings develop by coördination into clear consciousness, and the organised memory-structures form a more and more definite basis of psychic life, constituting a certain character, which when it reaches the domain of human life, is called personality.

APPERCEPTION AND WILL.

The question has been raised whether or not apperception is an act of the will; and the answer depends upon the meaning we attach to the word "will."

The most elementary kind of a will is to be found in the spontaneity of the simplest processes of nature. The actions and reactions of chemicals, the ether vibrations of light and electricity, and also the gravitation of a stone are motions that take place because the moving object possesses a certain quality which under special conditions makes it act in a certain way. These motions are self-motions or spontaneous motions. In this sense Schopenhauer uses the word "will."

By "will," however, we generally understand a peculiar kind of spontaneity, i. e., of the inherent quality of things which makes them move: will is the spontaneity only of intelligent beings. A tendency to pass into motion is called will only when it is accompanied by consciousness. Will is the incipient motion, the motive cause of which is a representative image (generally called motor idea) in the agent's mind; the object represented in this representative image being the aim or end to be attained.

Primitive apperception is a spontaneous action, the act of apperception bring the outcome of the peculiar qualities of the acting organism. It is an activity of the feeling substance: it is an apprehending and not merely a passive state of receiving impressions.

The peculiar qualities of an organism, which make apperception possible, are (1) psychical, for the memory-structures are endowed with sentiency, and (2) mental, for they possess representative value, they are endowed with meaning. Thus apperception is (in its primitive appearance, and of course in a very rudimentary way) at once a psychical and a mental process. But it does not become an act of will until the memory-structures grow strong and independent enough to exercise a choice and give preference to a certain kind of sense-impressions. By the neglect of other sense impressions all available sentiency is focussed upon one object or upon the search for one kind of object. This phenomenon, best observable in the hunt for food, is called attention, and attention is "apperception guided by will."

Whether or not amœbas and protozoa exhibit an elementary will when hunting for food is simply a question of terminology. According to Schopenhauer they do; according to the customary usage of the term, they do not. Their tissues demand a restoration of their waste products and they seek to satisfy this want. Their tendencies are processes of much higher complexity than the affinities of chemical substances, but there is no radical difference between the two actions. Prof. Max Verworn has proved that the protrusion of pseudopods in the amœba is caused by their chemotropy for oxygen, while their contraction, i. e. the return of the plasma to the nuclear substance, after an irritation of some kind which changes their chemical constitution, is due to a chemotropy for the nuclear substances. Their motions are tendencies; they are not actions of a will. We can speak of a will as soon as the irritation which causes the contraction of living substance is a commotion possessing representative value. There must be memory-structures present which not only feel the need of a restoration of the waste products in the tissues of the organism but have also a recollection of its prior satisfaction. This recollection is the primitive form of a motor idea. It serves as a stimulus to the motor organs of the organism to hunt for food. Thus the cause of the action is a mental state, and the action is planned, however vaguely. The aim of the action is the realisation of the motor-idea. There is no action of the will without either a motive, which is the motor idea, or without an end in view or purpose, which is the object represented by the motor idea.

That there is no definite line of demarcation where

tendencies become purposive acts of will is a matter of course, which, as in all analogous cases of evolutionary products, detracts nothing from the distinction to be made between these lower and higher phenomena of organised life.

IDEAS AND THE LIFE OF IDEAS.

Perceptions are the simplest acts of soul-life. But in the course of evolution a higher activity of soul-life springs from them, as soon as sounds are employed to designate certain composite pictures. These sound-symbols create a new sphere of mental life, with higher possibilities. Meaning-endowed sound-symbols are called "words," and the mechanism of words or articulate speech creates the domain of rational thought, which in its highest perfection is called science.

The meanings inherent in words and combinations of words are called ideas.

And what wonderful things ideas are—these highest kinds of meaning-freighted feelings! Every idea possesses an individuality of its own. Ideas grow and develop; they migrate from one brain into another, being transferred through the word-symbols of spoken or written language. Ideas adapt themselves to new environments; they struggle among themselves; some of them are victorious, others succumb. Some are exterminated, others survive. Those that survive suffer changes from assimilation among themselves. Some are powerful, others are weak, and a few assume dominion over their companions.

Ideas are real living beings: each one of them possesses a special individuality, and all of them are, as it were, citizens of that wonderful commonwealth called "the soul."

It has been said that states, churches, and other superindividual beings do not exist. We do not intend to discuss that problem now; but it appears that ideas would have at least the same right to deny the existence of human personalities, for a human personality is merely a society of ideas.

We may compare ideas (without going astray or being fantastical) to real persons. At least the idea we have of persons is after all the most appropriate simile we have to characterise their being. Think only of moral ideas, of ideals, of religious sentiments! They enter the souls of men and take hold of their entire existence often in spite of their will. And what a profound truth lies in the dogma of resurrection! Jesus the crucified has actually risen from the dead. Historical investigations have been made as to whether the apparitions of Christ as seen by his disciples, according to the Gospels, were not hallucinations; and the possibility of his bodily resurrection has been denied. It is true, and let it be true, that corpses cannot be revived. But what of that? We need not mind the fate of the body in the face of the truth that the soul possesses immortal life. Christ is actually a living presence in humanity, and his spirit was, and is still, the most dominating power in the evolution of mankind. The dogmatist, so called, and exactly so his adversary, the infidel, so called, imagine that Christianity must be a fraud unless it can be proved that the corpse of Jesus became reanimated. The conception of both the orthodox and the infidel is materialistic; both overlook the reality and importance of soul-life.

Ye of little faith and of still less understanding! It is a pagan notion to build a religion on the resurrection of corpses. True religion is based upon the immortality of the soul; and the immortality of the soul is no mere phrase, no empty allegory, no error or fraud: it is a fact provable by science; it is a reality without which no higher soul-life, no progress, no evolution would be possible: it is the corner-stone of religion and the basis of ethics.

PSYCHOLOGICAL TERMS.

In consideration of the importance of a clear, well-defined, and consistent terminology, we present the following psychological definitions and explanations:

Feeling is a state in which existence is, be it ever so dimly, aware of itself.

Sense-impression is the immediate and bodily effect of an event upon a sentient being.

Sensation is the feeling that takes place when a sense-impression is made. It is the sense-impression felt. Sensations are the simplest psychical facts and the ultimate units of our conscious subjectivity. They are, as it were, the atoms of our soul.

Sentiment is the degree of intensity as well as the pleasurableness and painfulness of feelings, which, as it were, give color to them.

Feelings, when strongly tinged with sentiment and liable to lead to action, are called *emotions*.

Traces are such modifications of the feeling substance produced by sense-impressions as persist.

Memory is that quality of sentient substance by virtue of which sense-impressions leave traces.

Memories are the feelings of the various traces as revived.

Image is the common name given to sensations and to the traces of sensations, which latter, when revived are felt again, and, as such, are called "memory-images." There are visual images, acoustic images, images of taste, of smell, of touch, and of temperature.

Composite images are combinations of the traces of many sense-impressions of one and the same or a similar kind, superimposed one upon another.

Perception is the feeling that attends the entrance of a sense-impression into the composite image of its class.

Percept is a sensation perceived.

Every perception is an elementary judgment. It is equivalent to a verdict that a sense-impression belongs to the class of traces among which it is registered.

By *person* we understand the totality of the memory-structures and composite images, interrelated among each other in an individual organism.

An isolated sensation, viz., a sensation which has not become a perception, which has not been registered in its respective composite image, may be called a feeling, but it certainly is not felt by the person who has the sensation. Feelings *are felt* by being interrelated, and the interrelation of feelings alone can produce perception. When a perception is become interrelated with the most important memory-images of a person, including the idea that represents the person, it is called *apperception*.

The peculiar feature which is the characteristic of all the various apperceptions is called *consciousness*. Thus consciousness is feeling systematised or focussed in a centre. It is a coördination of sentient images and an intensification of sentiment.

The pronoun "I" stands for the person of the speaker as a whole, and its Latin equivalent, "ego," has been used to denote the unity of a person as it appears in consciousness.

Ever since we reached an understanding of the nature of perception and apperception, the ego has ceased to be a mystery.

*   *   *

The objects of the surrounding world (whatever may be their other differences) must obviously differ in form, and this difference of form naturally produces an analogous difference of sense-impressions, of sensations and feelings. This accounts for the various kinds of feeling, which are appropriately called *forms of feeling*.

Memory-traces, being of various forms, analogous to the various forms of objects, come to represent or symbolise that class of objects or events through contact with which they have originated. They acquire meaning; and their feelings, having acquired meaning, are called *sentient symbols*.

Ideas are the meanings of sentient symbols.

Thought or *thinking* is the interaction that takes place among sentient symbols.

Impulses are feelings which tend to action.

Passions are strong sentiments tending to action.

Will is a conscious impulse, brought about after a longer or shorter deliberation by a consensus of the most powerful ideas.

Purpose is an idea willed, i. e., a plan, the execution of which is determined.

Action is the motion of an organism, performed after conscious deliberation; it is purposive motion.

The term *psychical* applies to feelings as feelings.

The term *mental* applies to thought-operations.

The term *spiritual* applies to the representative value of feelings.

Soul is the name given to the system of sentient symbols as a totality.

Soul, mind, spirit, and character are synonyms with different shades of meaning.

When using the term *soul*, we think mainly of the feeling element and the various forms of feelings, of sentiments, passions, and emotions.

When using the word *mind*, we think principally of mental or intellectual qualities, of thought-operations, logical conclusions, judgments, or ideas.

When using the word *spirit*, we leave out of sight all the corporeal relations of a feeling organism, and think mainly of the meaning residing in psychic symbols, in ideas and ideals.

When using the word *character*, we think of the peculiar nature of the impulses, desires, inclinations, and will of a man.

* * *

Faculty is the collective name given to the various features of our psychical, mental, or spiritual operations.

The old doctrine, that the soul possesses faculties which have their distinct seats and well-defined provinces, is exploded. Every faculty is a collective term framed to designate a certain kind of mental activity, or a certain quality of thought-operations. Thus we speak of memory, of cognition, of judgment, of imagination, of attention, etc., as faculties.

Imagination is (1) the free play of ideas; (2) that quality of thinking beings which allows images or ideas to enter into all possible combinations.

Attention is the concentration of the soul; it is that state of mind in which one single impulse or will predominates, either suppressing all other impulses, or making them subservient.

Cognition is conscious and deliberate perception. It denotes especially all complex processes of perception, the analysis of complex ideas, and the arrangement of their elements in the respective categories to which they belong. Comprehension is the distinct perception of that which is alike in two or several apparently heterogeneous phenomena, thus rendering possible a description of their essential features in a common formula, called natural law.

Intellect is the presence of such conditions as make cognition possible.

Intelligence is the ability of practically employing one's intellect.

Understanding is that quality which makes thinking beings find explanations. It is the recognition of changes as transformations, or, in other words, the tracing of causation.

Reason is, (1) that quality of sentient beings which makes thought-operations possible. In short, it is the faculty of thinking.

We have parenthetically to add that the ability to draw conclusions from premises, which is one of the most important functions of reason, is called *judgment*.

Being especially methodical thinking, reason is, in

its strict and proper sense, (2) the method of thinking, the purpose of which is the economy of thought.

Reason also denotes the means by which economy of thought is accomplished. Economy of thought being possible through a systematisation of the uniformities of experience, reason means (3) abstract thought, or the ability of making and employing abstractions, and also those most important products of abstraction—generalisations.

Lastly, we understand by reason (4) the norm or criterion of thought-operations, by which we judge their correctness.

RELIGION.

CHRISTIANITY.

There are two kinds of Christianity: the one is the spirit of the lesson taught mankind in the life and death of Christ, the other is a church organisation which historically originated with Jesus and claims that the acceptance of certain dogmas is the indispensable condition of salvation. The former Christianity is the very soul of our civilisation, the latter an embarrassing dead weight on the feet of mankind, obstructing all progress and higher development. The Jesus of the Gospels speaks in parables, but his followers prefer to have the dead letter to believe in, for, (as says Mephistopheles in Goethe's "Faust,):

> "*An Worte lässt sich trefflich glauben,*
> *Von einem Wort lässt sich kein Iota rauben.*"
>
> [On words 'tis excellent believing,
> No word can ever lose a jot from thieving.]

It is so convenient to take parables literally. While it is troublesome to understand the living spirit, it is very easy to believe in the dead letter. The letter of the Christian parables has been formulated by the fathers and ancient bishops into a system of beliefs, which are our confessions of faith so called. There is a wonderful logicality about them, and they are admirably constructed in their joints; but let us not forget that they are subject to criticism, for they are the work of man, not of God.

The authors who fashioned these confessions of faith stepped boldly forward and said to the people, "These be thy gods, O Israel"; and there are to day many who still believe that the historical documents of their religion are the words of absolute truth. But civilised mankind has outgrown these old formulations of past creeds.

We do not deny that parables are good things. On the contrary, we believe that parables are the vehicles which convey truth. All our words are symbols, and we communicate our ideas through symbols. Greek poets symbolise beauty as Aphrodite, time as Kronos, wisdom as Athene, etc. There is no objection to this method; but he who ingenuously believes in the symbol itself, and not in the meaning conveyed by the symbol, is a pagan, an idolater, a heathen; and the Christian who believes in the literal truth of his symbolic books, parables, and confessions of faith, stands upon the same standpoint: he also is a pagan, and we may characterise him as a Christian pagan.

Christianity, the true Christianity, is a moral factor in the world,—nay, it is *the* moral factor in the evolution of mankind.

Christianity teaches us that life is serious; it is not mere play. We do not live for happiness, but for the performance of duties ; and the performance of our duties can be perfect only if the main-spring of our actions is love—love of that which is our duty, love of our neighbor, love even of our enemy. And our path naturally leads *per aspera ad astra, per crucem ad lucem*, through self-sacrifice to victory. This truth, mythologically and allegorically expressed in the Gospels in so many various ways, is a truth that science corroborates more and more. Let the mythology of Christianity go ; the significance with which its symbols are filled is true !

The moral spirit of Christianity exemplified in Christ's life and teachings is the same as that which is taught by science and is revealed to us in the facts of existence.

The churches of to-day are not what they ought to be. If Jesus of Nazareth were in our midst to-day, and if he came unto his own, they, most assuredly, would receive him not. Would not the scene in the temple be repeated? Would He not again cast out those that sell and buy, and overturn the tables of the money-changers? And would not afterwards the result also be the same, or similar?

While our churches are not what they ought to be, we yet recognise that they are not without moral aspirations. The light of science begins to enter under the influence of a deeper insight into the foundations of religion and morality, the struggle for the ideal asserts itself, broadening their faith and developing it out of paganism into a cosmic religion of true catholicity.

Our visible churches possess the ideal of the invisible church, and the religion of the invisible church is Christ's religion of morality, of sacrifice, of love ; it is the religion of science ; it is the religion of truth.

IDOLATRY.

Idolatry, or the worship of images, is the attributing of divine honors to the symbols that represent God or are thought to represent God.

The most primitive kind of idolatry is fetishism, as practised among savages ; the most modern kind is that which substitutes ideas for stone or wood figures. These modern ideas, however, are sometimes incomparably more wretched than the carved idols of the African savage ; where the latter are ill-shaped and ugly, the former are ill-conceived and erroneous. Both are alike products of poorest workmanship ; both are treated with a ridiculous awe ; both are made the recipients of divine honors which are paid with the more scrupulous attention, to the fetish-images the more rotten and hideous they are, to the fetish-ideas the more errors they contain.

We look upon the bigoted dogmatist who places his particular man-shaped creed above God's universal revelation in nature, as a man deeply entangled in paganism. Christianity has become a fetish to him ;

he finds it easier to worship Christ than to follow him and he must be regarded as much an idolater as many pagans before him.

The dogmatist's idolatry is mainly due to indolence, and finds its explanation in the conservatism and the *vis inertiæ* of tradition. His fault is lack of courage. He does not feel independent enough to advance on the road of progress. He adopts the letter of Christianity and forgets its spirit. He is of interest to the student as a living fossil, representing a certain historical stage in the religious evolution of mankind. He is a religious dodo—a survival destined to speedy extinction on the approach of civilisation.

The case is somewhat different with certain other idea-worshippers, whose idolatry, however, is no less inexcusable. There are men, sufficiently bold to break the spell of traditional authority, who, despite their good intentions, still relapse into the most abject idolatry. They make themselves images woven of the delicate threads of thought. Such idea-worshippers are idolaters not from lack of courage but from lack of understanding. They are not afraid to break with traditional beliefs. Their deficiency is that they lack insight.

Because it is absurd to worship any clear and sound ideas that serve real practical purposes, these idea-worshippers employ such thoughts only as are unfit to be used otherwise. The most absurd and self-contradictory ideas, such as the absolute, the unknowable, the infinite, are the fittest objects of idolatry. Ideas which people do not understand make their heads swim. So they sink down upon their knees, and being in this position, they have simply to follow the old inherited habit of worshipping.

Idolatry begins where rational thought ends. Thus as soon as a man is hopelessly entangled in a problem which he is too weak-minded to solve, he declares, "This is a holy ground, take off your shoes and worship that which you cannot understand."

It is the peculiarity of idolaters to worship that which they do not understand *because* they do not understand it.

The worship in spirit and in truth, of which Christ spoke, is the doing of the will of God, i. e., obedience to the moral law of nature. However, the worship that consists in genuflection and "Lord, Lord" saying, is pure adoration, and a worship of self-humiliation, of fawning and cringing debases us and shows how human the God is whom we revere.

The religion of adoration is idolatry; it is an inferior kind of religion which substitutes prayers for actions and recommends flattery as the means of gaining the favor of God. But the will of God cannot be changed by adulation.

The will of God is written in the unalterable laws of nature, especially in the moral laws through which alone human society can exist. These laws contain blessings and curses; and God's will is that we ourselves shall work out the blessings of his laws. To pray that God should not do his will, that he should alter the laws of the universe, make exceptions in our favor, or that he should accomplish what it is our duty to accomplish is to reverse the prayer of Christ, which teaches us to say, "Thy will be done."

To look upon prayer in any other light than as a self-discipline, is to share the superstition of the medicine-man who still believes in the spells by which he thinks he is able to change the course of nature; and the worship of adoration is as idolatrous, as the belief that God is a big human being who is pleased to witness our abject and self-humiliating adulation is pagan. Adoration can be tolerated only as an educational method of attuning by a kind of dramatic symbolism the souls of the immature to the harmony of the moral world-order. It is a substitute only for those who do not as yet understand the worth of the moral laws of life which can be revealed in their full glory and sanctity only in the religion of science.

* * *

A comparison between the old dogmatism, the idolatry of traditional symbols, and modern agnosticism, the idolatry of the Unknowable (both being idolatries of a different kind) shows the great superiority of the former. The God of the dogmatist is anthropomorphic; but after all, this image of God contains some excellent features of true divinity. The decalogue is rational and practical in the best sense of the words. There is no nonsense about it, no confusion of thought, no absurdity—if but the allegorical nature of religious symbols be kept in mind. The God who is regarded as the authority of the moral law is not worshipped because he is unknowable, but because his commandments, which are obviously knowable, are true, because those who neglect his commandments will bring down upon themselves and others the curses of the moral laws of nature, while those who obey them will change the curses into blessings. There is substance in the old religions. But there is no substance in agnosticism.

We grant that the dogmatist's conception who takes the allegorical part of the parables in the literal sense and often regards it as their most important truth, is a miserable superstition and real paganisn. But the worship of actually erroneous ideas is worse still. The idea-fetishes are too shadowy, too vague, too misty to receive any other attention than the critic's, under whose analysis they will have to give up the ghost.

Briefly : the idolatry of the dogmatists is an anachronism, the idolatry of the idea-worshipper is a degeneration, and you, my dear reader, if you find it necessary to avoid the Scylla of the former, do not fall into the Charybdis of the latter.

THE RELIGION OF SCIENCE.

Our scientists apply the best methods of observation and the most rigorous criticism, in order to make, in their diverse fields of inquiry, a correct and systematically arranged statement of facts. The importance of science as the basis of human civilisation in its broadest scope and as the condition of further progress is now well-nigh universally recognised. It is not doubted for industrial invention, nor for art, nor for politics, nor economics. It is doubted only for the most important province of human life—viz., for religion.

Religion is the basis of conduct. All those ideas are religious which regulate man's actions and support him in the vicissitudes of life. Religion is the ethical power in humanity, being the norm of human aspirations, the authority of rules and laws and injunctions, and the lofty ideal that sanctifies existence with its joys and griefs, consecrating every single individual to a higher purpose than himself.

It is a very strange fact that the importance of science, which is admitted in every other field, could have been doubted for religion. The reason, however, is obvious to him who is familiar with the history of the various religions. Religious doctrines are such valuable possessions that their keepers always wanted to shelter them from danger; they were anxious to guard them as a sacred inheritance and hand them down to future generations inviolate. They wanted to protect the holy treasures from the vagaries of the scientist groping about after the truth and often failing to find it. So they declared that religion was independent of science and had nothing whatever to do with it. They did not see that scientists are not always identical with science, exactly as priests are not always the true prophets of religion. Thus they founded religion upon the authority of tradition, instead of upon the rock of ages, which is truth—provable truth. They went so far as to call human tradition a divine revelation and to discredit that grand apocalypse which lies open to every one of us—nature. The absurd was sanctified; and reason, the divine spark in man that kindles the torch to enlighten his path, was scorned as an *ignis fatuus*.

Yet, after all, what is religion but the trust in truth, the search for truth, and living the truth! Shall we, indeed, use the best methods of searching for the truth in all domains except in the most important domain, in religion? To suppress the truth where it is our duty to speak it out, is regarded as equivalent to a lie; and rightly so! Shall we suppress the search for truth in religion, the essence of which is, or rather ought to be, truth, and which is transformed into abject superstition when errors are enshrined upon the altar of truth? Religion is to us inseparable from truth; and the search for truth is our holiest duty.

All religions which do not aspire to be based upon truth are superstitions. There is but one true religion, which is the religion of truth.

When we speak of the Religion of Science, we wish to indicate that our idea of truth is different from the ideas of those who believe in the duality of truth.

Truth is no Janus-head with two faces. It is an error that something may be true in science which is untrue in religion, that twice two is four only in the multiplication tables, but not in the catechism, that there are other methods of finding out or proving the truth for the religious prophet than for the savant—in short, that science is human truth, while religion is divine truth.

Truth is truth. There is but one truth and that one truth is divine. Man is divine in so far as he partakes of the truth, and science, the methodical search for truth, is the most important vehicle to help man to progress, to grow, to develop, and to become more and more divine.

All our religions have been founded as religions of truth. Jesus of Nazareth, the Messiah and Christ that made the new covenant with mankind upon the foundation of love, has nowhere, so far as our maturest biblical criticism can pierce, established any dogma, and least of all the absurd theory that above the truth there is another truth, and that this higher truth standing in contradiction to scientific truth must be believed in because it appears, or even because it is, absurd.

Science is holy. It is the religious duty of the scientist to search for truth in *all* fields, philosophy, ecclesiastical history, and biblical research not excepted. And it is a religious duty of the clergy to respect science. They need not accept the hypotheses of scientists, but they must revere truth whenever proved to be truth, for truth is sacred whatever it be. There is a divinity in mathematics, of which the modern idolater of dogmatic Christianity has no idea.

We can nowhere, either in practical life or in our religious sentiments and convictions, dispense with a rational inquiry into truth; that is to say, religion is inseparable from science.

*　*　*

Religion is not identical with science; religion is the enthusiasm of applying that knowledge, of whose truth and potency we are unwaveringly convinced, to practical life. Science is in many respects opposed to and very different from religion; for science is of the head, and religion is of the heart. Yet science and religion should keep abreast of each other. They should be allied. One should be the complement of the other. Schiller says in his "Philosophical Letters":

> *"Lasst uns hell denken, so werden wir feurig lieben."*
> [Let us think clearly and we shall love warmly.]

Philosophy, science, experience, reason, all the best methods of inquiry at our command, must be called upon to guide our feelings and our religious enthusiasm.

There is a close connection between thought and feeling, so close that the tenor of our feelings will also have its effects upon our thought, and *vice versa*. Only he whose heart is hopelessly chilled by ill-will or egotism will be little benefited by the enlightenments of rational insight or science. Science may help to show him the futility of ill-will and the irrationality of egotism, and thus slowly cure him of his irreligious disposition. But upon the whole, Faust's words will remain true:

> "*Wenn ihr's nicht fühlt, ihr werdet's nicht erjagen.*"
> [If you don't feel it, you will never know it.]

*   *   *

So long as the scientist doubts, he inquires, but as soon as he has found the truth, he proclaims it and solicits the criticism of his fellow-workers. This same method is applicable to religion. He who doubts, must inquire; and he who believes he has found the truth, must allow his fellowmen to criticise him, to point out what they regard as errors, and to let his views be tested by criticism.

Is it not pusillanimous to be afraid of criticism? And is it true that we have to protect truth against criticism? If our religion is true, why prevent investigation?

It is said that the scientist may err, and that his critics may err, and that errors are more powerful than the truth. Yet we answer with Milton:

"Whoever knew truth put to the worse in a free and open encounter?"

Those who err, may be more powerful than those who speak the truth. Those who speak the truth may be put to death; nay, they have often been put to death; and errors are more plentiful and fertile than the truth. Nevertheless, truth is more powerful and will in the end always prevail.

Science is calm, impartial, rigorous; and many warm-hearted men and women have a dislike for science, because of its austerity. They should know, that while the search for truth must be made by cool-headed thinkers, the application of truth demands enthusiasm and fervid zeal. The religion of science is the most elevating and noble ideal of mankind.

The old religions have become dear to their adherents, and justly so. For all the religions upon earth are intended to be religions of truth—the same truth that scientific truth is made of. And they are the more orthodox (that is, possessing the right doctrines) and the more catholic (that is, universally valid) and the freer from superstitions (that is, freer from absurdities believed to be exempt from scientific criticism), the nearer they come to their common ideal, which is the religion of science.

We do not preach the religion of science to destroy the old religions; we preach it that the old religions may avoid false dogmatism, and that they may adopt the method of science, which is a systematic search for truth without reserve and open to criticism. This will widen the narrowest sectarianism into a cosmical religion, as broad as the universe, as reliable as the revelations of God in the book of nature, and as sacred as the truths of science.

We expect that all the various sects of mankind

will by and by acknowledge this principle of the religion of science. Indeed, they will have to! For how can they otherwise stand the bracing air of progress? They need not give up the peculiarities that are not in contradiction to truth. They can, and let us hope they will, preserve their character, their organisation, their brotherly love, their zeal for their special tradition and form of religion. Only, let them drop the pagan features of their worship as soon as, in the light of science, they recognise them as pagan.

This is our confession of faith : We trust in truth, and claim that truthfulness (i. e., fidelity to truth generally and especially also to exact, provable, scientific truth) is the condition of all religion. And this religious ideal is holy to us. We cling to it with enthusiasm and leave it as the most sacred inheritance to future generations.

INDEX.

Absolute, its definitions, 127, 128, 131; its idolatrous worship, 127, 128, 200.

Absolute, certainty, meaning of the expression, 131; existence, source of the idea, 132; monarchy, 131; zero of temperature, 131.

Abstract idea of God not prevalent, 147.

Abstract ideas, based on sense-impressions, 135; compared to checks, 134; do not represent things in themselves, 122; not explained by association, 175; not unreal, 126; represent features of reality, 1, 122; symbols of reality, 34, 121, 133, 134.

Abstract thought, exclusive prerogative of man, 123; generalisations its product, 125; not so vivid as intuition, 126; the meaning of reason, 195.

Abstraction, a fundamental psychic function, 127; derivation of the word, 122; impossible to animals, 78; its functions, 72, 126; its nature, 123, 125; scholastic use of term, 122, 123; the condition of formal thought, 78; the function of reason, 194; the method of thought, 118; the source of mathematical data, 101; various uses of term, 124.

Abstracts, of reality called subjectivity and objectivity, 17; not entities or essences, 133; not sensations, 127; the particuiarly human in man, 134.

Absurd, its sanctification by priests, 205.

Acoustic images, 190.

Action, its definition, 192; chemical, a form of will, 184.

Actions, estimated by motives, 163; should be inspired by love, 198; the expression of nature or character, 160, 161, 165, 166; without knowledge mere reflexes, 39.

Adoration, idolatrous, 201, 202; tolerable only as education, 202.

African idolatry compared with that of civilisation, 199.

Agnosticism, arises from confusion of thought, 120; avoided by monism, 177; compared with dogmatism, 202; fatal to philosophy, iv; of Comtism, 2; should be abandoned, 4; the outcome of nominalism, 104; the outcome of associationalism, 177; without substance, 203.

Αἰτία distinguished from ἀρχή, 143.

Algebra, a rigidly formal science, 79, 110, 111; tridimensionality of space a problem of, 99.

Algebraic symbols to be considered words, 39.

Alimentation a property of cells, 168.

All, its identity with God, 49; the only absolute, 121.

Amœba, cause of its movements, 186; its exhibition of will, 185.

Anachronism, dogmatism an, 203.

Analysis, of experience, cause of single facts, 105; of sensations, by abstract thought, 126.

Analytics of Aristotle, quoted, 52.

Angles, their properties, 84.

Animal brain, to nominalists a picture of reality, 104.

INDEX.

Animals, how man is distinguished from, 118; incapable of abstract thought, 78, 123.

Annihilation would be perplexing, 156.

Anschauung, its definition, 9, 127; contrasted with abstract thought, 126; its data the realities of life, 135; represents objects, 14; the true meaning of intuition, 125; synonym for atsight, 133.

Anthropomorphic view of nature, 170.

Anthropomorphism, idolatrous, 202; its truths, 202.

Antinomy involved in finitude of space, 97.

Aphrodite, a symbol of beauty, 197.

Apocalypse of nature, 26, 205.

A posteriori, axioms so considered by Mill, 59; history of term, 62, 63, 65; Kant's view of, 31, 33, 66; popular and philosophic uses of term, 73.

Appearance, not a sham, 21.

Apperception, its definition, 185, 191; at first spontaneous, 185; both mental and psychical, 185; explains ego, 191; its conditions, 185; its relations to will, 184, 185; the function of consciousness, 182, 183.

Application, a function of science, 153; of sciences, a function of philosophy, 45.

A priori, definitions of the, 61, 73; an important element of knowledge, 88; axioms as considered by Kant, 59; better called formal, 77; cause of aversion to the, 68; dangers of the idea, 68; history of term, 62, 63, 64; Kant's conception of the, 31, 33, 37, 66, 67; its importance, 35, 73; its origin, 36; the most fundamental problem, 73.

A priori, character of mathematical reasoning, 56, 101; construction of triangles, 86; determinability of certain truths, 107; determination the problem of reason, 106; knowledge, its different kinds, 64.

Apriorism, of Kant, iii, 177; reconciled with empiricism, 70.

Aquinas, St. Thomas, his definition of truth, 46.

Arbitrariness, of existence, 102; of geometrical constructions, 82; of maxims, 80.

Aristotelian books, their authorship, 145.

Aristotle, cited, 52. 62, 63; his definition of axiom, 52; his theory of the source of knowledge, 28; his views of causation, 143, 144, 150, 156.

Arithmetic, a rigidly formal science, 79, 110, 111; illustrates logical necessity, 115; not a mere fiction, 134.

Ἀρχή distinguished from αἰτία 143.

Asceticism, product of false monism, 24.

Aspiration, exists in all worlds, 171; identical with natural living, 171; of moral endeavor, 167; religion its norm, 204; the grandest of nature's tendencies, 171; the universal law of life, 169.

Association, of ideas, 173, 174, 175; not the cause of reason, 117; not the fundamental principle of philosophy, 175.

Association philosophy, contrasted with Kantianism, 177; criticism of, 173; its principles, 175; its outcome scepticism, agnosticism, or materialism, 177; its view of causation, 176.

Assumption of universality, how justified, 104.

Assumptions, arbitrary constructions not, 82; in mathematics and mechanics, 90; in nominalism, 105; not necessary to formal sciences, 111.

Astronomy might be considered a branch of logic, 44.

Atheists, their view of universe, 129.

Athene, a symbol of wisdom, 197.

Atsight, meaning of the word, 9.

Atsights, a synonym for phenomena, 133; basis of abstract ideas, 126; represent objects, 14; the data of experience, 9, 125; their elements, 10.

Attention, its definition, 185, 193, 194; its function in cognition, 183.

Authority, for conduct, 167, 170; of reason, 175; the practical idea of God, 147, 170.
Awareness, the stuff of consciousness, 10.
Axiom, definition of the term, 51; Newton's misapplication of the word, 52; recognised by Aristotle, 52; the word not used by Euclid, 52.
Axiom of consistency, 109; of parallels, 95, 110.
Axioms, all theorems considered such by Schopenhauer, 54, 55; arbitrary constructions not, 82; belief in, a superstition, 51; derived from conception of space, 56, 80; how their nature should be determined, 60; inadmissible in science and philosophy, 55, 58, 67, 79; not the basis of investigation, 58; rigidly formal truths not, 61; supposed dilemma regarding, 59; their need of demonstration, 131.

Bacilli, their multiplication, 115.
Bacon, Lord Francis, his theory of knowledge, 28.
Bad exists only in mentality, 22.
Ball, Sir Robert, his views on space, 95, 96, 97.
Barometer, illustrates causality, 142, 143.
Basic problems of philosophy, declared by Comtists insoluble, 2.
Beauty, symbolised by Aphrodite, 133, 197.
Begetting, represented by same word as knowing, 38.
Being, conscious of itself, 10; identical with soul and thought, 25; its true nature exhibited in forces, 162.
Biblical criticism, its results, 206.
Blessings to be gained by obedience, 202, 203.
Body, an abstract idea, 4, 19; inseparable from soul, 23; its essence the soul, 23, 25; its resurrection unimportant, 188.
Book of nature, God's revelation, 209.

Boxes for storing abstracts, 119.
Brahman monism, its one-sidedness and fatal results, 23.
Brain, composite photography in the, 178; filled with paths of association, 173.

Categories, a system of relational ideas, 78.
Catholicity, Christianity becoming a true, 78; the religion of science, 78.
Causa æquat effectum, disproved, 150, 152.
Causa, distinguished from *ratio*, 143.
Causa sui an absurdity, 145.
Causation, Aristotle's analysis of it revised, 143, 144; a transformation of matter and energy, 144, 152, 155, 194; denied by the association philosophy, 176, 177; confirmed by science, 156; confused notions of, 145; does not affect substance, 152; governs character and properties, 166; implies necessity, 160; its branches, 148; its idea not a mere association of its sentiments, 175; its universality, 18; means conservation of matter and energy, 155; not a mystery, 153; not a self-evident principle, 148; not mere succession, 152; notion of, its basis, 148; Schopenhauer's view of, 147; the test problem, 137.
Cause, its definition, 137, 138; and effect, law of, 167; continues to exist in effect, 142; distinguished from *raison d'être*, 143; efficient the only true, 144; identified by Lewes with law, 149; never equal to its effect, 152; the idea a noumenon, 148; the object of superstitious reverence, 159, 160.
Causes, their nature, 153; always both efficient and final, 156; always motions or events, 150; are facts, 149; Aristotle's classification of, 143; misconceived by Hume, 151; to be distinguished from reason, 139.
Cells, their coöperative organisation, 168.

Centralising of feeling, the function of consciousness, 182.

Century Dictionary, quoted, 123, 124, 133.

Certainty, based on formal laws, 114; its formal operations, 115.

Chance, nature not governed by, 158.

Changes are all transformations, 194.

Chaos would result from inconsistency of reason, 110.

Character, its definition, 193; analogous to properties of things, 166; free action its expression, 160, 165; implies determinism, 163; its importance, 166; of nature, 161, 165; the essence of personality, 184.

Chemical, action and reaction a form of will, 184; affinity, resemblance of protozoan activities to, 186; analysis, mathematical demonstration compared with, 74; substances, an illustration of character, 165; substances, their changes of shape, 158.

Chemistry, its field of inquiry, 43.

Chemotrophy, exhibited in amœba, 186.

Christ, a living presence in humanity, 188; cited, 50, 201; easier to worship than to follow, 200; his new covenant, 206; his prayer, 209; his resurrection, 188; true Christianity his spirit, 194; true morality of his life and teachings, 198.

Christian mythology, its view of divine paternity, 98.

Christianity, dogmatists have only its letter, 200; false, an obstacle to progress, 196; its meaning true, 198; its relation to moral truths, 27; its mission, 49; its moral spirit scientific, 198; its mythology unimportant, 198; its two kinds, 196; not dependent on physical resurrection, 189; the moral factor of evolution, 197; the soul of civilisation, 196.

Churches, have the ideal of the invisible church, 199; not what they should be, 198.

Circle, equality of its peripheral angles, 84.

Circumstances, distinguished from causes, 137.

Civilisation, fatal to dogmatism, 200; increases happiness, 6: science its basis, 204; true Christianity its soul, 196.

Clergy, their duty to respect science, 206.

Cognition, its definition, 181, 193, 194; its conformity to objects, 87; its simplest form, 181; Kant's view of, 35, 66; not mysterious, 181; presupposes general notions, 181, 182; the origin of knowledge, 38.

Coherence among facts of experience, 72, 104, 105.

Cold, its perception an abstraction, 127.

Colors, reducible to three, 100.

Combinations and separations compose nature, 111.

Commissural fibres of brain, their function, 173.

Common notions, in mathematics and mechanics, 52, 58, 80,

Composite images, definition of, 190; the elements of soul, 178, 179.

Composite memories, the means of generalisation, 175, 179.

Composite pictures symbolised by sound, 186.

Comprehension, its definition of, 155; the universe, how attainable, 102.

Compulsion, comparable to secondary motions, 161; distinguished from necessity, 160; illustrated in a magnet, 162, 163; one kind of determination, 164.

Comte, Auguste, his idea of philosophy, 45; his positivism an agnosticism, 2; his rejection of the *a priori*, 68.

Concentration of feeling in apperception, 183.

Concepts, not explained by association, 175.

Conduct, God its authority, 147; immoral, its penalty destruction, 170.

Confessions of faith, 53, 190, 196, 197, 210.

INDEX.

Conic sections, celestial bodies move in, 85.

Consciousness, its definition, 121, 182, 191; accompanies volition, 157, 184; dependent on memory, 183, 184; its function, 24, 173, 182, 184, 191; its relation to the unconditioned, 130; its states, the data of experience, 10; the characteristic of apperception, 191.

Consecration of the individual to high purpose, 204.

Consequence, correlative with reason, 140; distinguished from sequence, 141.

Conservation of matter and energy, 155, 166; of tradition, 200.

Consistency, of being, 102, 112; of mental operations, 56, 109.

Construction in geometry, 82, 83, 86, 91.

Contents of states of consciousness, 11.

Contiguity, association by, 173, 174.

Contrast, association by, 173, 174.

Coördination the function of consciousness, 182, 184, 291.

Corporeality, its perception an act of abstraction, 127.

Correctness distinguished from truth, 49.

Cosmic, nature of the world, 112; religion, 199, 207.

Cosmos, its revelation, 166.

Creation would be perplexing, 156.

Creeds, not to be placed above universal revelation, 199.

Criterion of *a priori* truths, 65; of thought-operations, 194.

Criticism, its value, 208; should be encouraged by religion, 209.

Criticism, of Bible, 206; of creeds, 197; of terms, 159.

Critique of Pure Reason, cited, 30, 32, 77, 86; Schurman's view of it, 75.

Crystallisation of chemical substances, 158.

Curses earned by disobedience to moral law, 203.

Curvature of space, 84, 95, 96.

Curved line, definitions of, 96, 97.

Data of experience, phenomena, 133; single sense-impressions, 74; states of consciousness, 10; the realities of life, 135; their elements, 9, 10.

Data of Psychology, Spencer's, cited, 120.

Decalogue rational and practical, 202.

Deductive reason, called *a priori*, 63.

Deeds, their immortality, 171.

Dependence of individual upon the whole, 171.

Descartes, his theory of innate ideas, 28; his use of objective in old sense, 13.

Descartes's Discourse, Huxley's address on, 120.

Design in nature, no conscious one, 158.

Destruction the penalty of sin, 170.

Determinableness, the problem of, 105, 106.

Determination of reason, 111.

Determinism, consistent with freedom, 160; not fatalism, 106.

Die lineale Ausdehnungslehre, cited, 54.

Die Theilung der Erde, cited, 45.

Dilemma, about nature of axioms, 59; of teleology, 158.

Dimensions, defined, 102; artificial, 95; problem of, 102.

Directions, infinite in space, 94.

Disobedience to God, immorality, 170; punished, 203.

Divinity, in mathematics, 207; of truth, 205; truth in dogmatic notions of, 202.

Doctrines, guarded by their keepers, 204.

Dodo, the dogmatist a religious, 200.

Dogmas, false Christianity a system of, 196; none established by Christ, 206.

Dogmatic religions compared with agnosticism, 203.

Dogmatism, compared with agnosticism, 200, 202; its mystery, 189; should be avoided by old religions, 209.

Dogmatists, living fossils, 200 : their idolatry, 199, 200, 203, 207 : their God anthropomorphic, 202 ; their literalism absurd, 203.

Doubt, leads to inquiry, 208.

Dreams, sensations, their reality, 20, 21.

Drobisch, cited, 124.

Dualism, leads to triunism, 101 ; none in subjectivity and objectivity, 17 ; outcome of associationalism, 175 ; outcome of one-sided monism, 29 ; supported by transcendentalism, 67; to be overcome by scientific progress, 4.

Dualistic idea of gravitation, 164.

Duality, of subject, and object not dualism, 17 ; of truth denied by Christ and science, 205, 206.

Duns Scotus, first to distinguish subject and object, 12, 13.

Duty, gives value to life, 198 ; implied by world-constitution, 167 ; made perfect by love, 198 ; of clergy to respect science, 206 ; of scientists to seek truth, 206.

Ear, its function an abstraction, 127.

Economy of thought, by systematisation of experience, 194.

Ecstasies, 26.

Effect, the idea a noumenon, 148.

Effects, always causal, 157 ; their nature, 137, 142, 144, 152, 153, 157.

Efficient cause, defined by Aristotle, 144, all causes such, 156.

Ego, its definition, 191 ; discovered by Kant, 68 ; explained by nature of apperception, 191; its attempted proof by transcendentalism, 67.

Egotism, an obstacle to scientific enlightenment, 207, 208 ; not the mainspring of right effort, 167.

Eighth axiom of Euclid, 57.

Electricity a form of will, 184.

Elements, constant change in their combinations, 166.

Eleventh axiom of Euclid, 57, 58.

Elliptic geometry, 80.

Emotions, defined, 190.

Empirically formal, defined, 79, 86.

Empiricism reconciled with apriorism, iii, 70.

Encyclopædia Britannica, cited, 60.

Energy, its conservation, 42, 155, 159 ; its relation to the unconditioned, 130 ; its transfer in audition, 142 ; not explanation of soul, 119; not matter, 121 ; transformed in causation, 152.

English school, its misunderstanding of the formal, 75.

Enjoyment not to be sought, 7.

Erkenntnissgrund, 148.

Error, its cause, 22 ; less potent than truth 208, 209 ; purely mental, 22, 48.

Essay on Human Understanding, cited, 28.

Eternity implied in existence, 94.

Ether vibrations a form of will, 184.

Ethical power in humanity, 204; principle indispensable to organisms, 169.

Ethics, how affected by subjectivism, 23 ; its basis, 4, 5, 189; the test of philosophy, 5.

Euclid, cited, 97 ; does not use the word axiom, 52 ; his common notions and postulates not axioms, 58, 60; his eleventh and twelfth axioms, 58 ; Schopenhauer's opinion of his demonstrations, 53.

Euclidean axioms denied by modern mathematicians, 95.

Euclidean geometry, its assumption, 57, 111; not only kind, 80, 109; purely formal, 79.

Euclidean space, an assumption, 55; its characteristics, 56, 57, 81; its construction, 57 ; its existence denied by Ball, 95.

Euclidean straight lines possible even if space is curved, 96.

Evenness of space, a negative quality, 98.

Events, causes of things, 137; explainable only as transformations, 36, 105, 156, 176 ; their necessity determinism, 106, 164.

Everything a cause and an effect, 151.

Evolution, Christ its dominating power, 189, 197; dependent on immortality, 189; does not tend to increase happiness, 6; dogmatists represent a certain stage of, 200; on other planets, 168; revelation of Saviour-God, 101; *sursum* its watchword, 171; tends to improve conditions, 166, 167.

Evolution, of formal thought, 78; of human faculties, 171; of mind a necessity, 20, 34; of religion, explained by philosophy, 5; of soul-life, 186.

Existence, absolute, source of the idea, 132; a cosmos not a medley, 112; appears to us arbitrary, 102; both subjective and objective, 15, 17; its nature, 10, 20, 88; objectivity of nature its apocalypse, 26.

Experience, accords with formal knowledge, 111; a psychic phenomenon, 43; axioms not dependent on, 59; basis of abstract ideas, 135; basis of science and philosophy, 9, 37, 43; caused by sense-impressions, 113; coherence among its facts, 71, 104, 105; confirms Christian morality, 198; its conditions, 26; its data, 72, 74, 135; its nature and functions, 25, 26, 34, 154, 207; its method, 78, 117; its problems solvable by philosophy, 137; its range widened by science, 42; its relation to knowledge, 31, 32, 33, 34; its universal features, 105, 117; methods of philosophy derived from, 51; represented by abstracts, 118; same nature as thought, 111; sole source of knowledge, 28, 69; systematisation of its uniformities, 194; the foundation of ethics, 170; the foundation of truth, 49; the medium of revelation, 37, 117; unnecessary for determining certain truths, 107; wrongly defined by associationalists, 177.

Experiments, their object, 166.

Explanation, a function of science, 153; definition of the word, 153, 154.

Extension, Huxley's view of, 120.

Eye, its function an abstraction, 127.

Facts, identified by Lewes with causes and laws, 149; pictured in sensations, 39; real or unreal, 47; single and concrete events, 149; the basis of all investigations, 2, 58, 90.

Faculties, their nature, 193.

Faith, broadened by science, 198; its importance, 167.

Falsehood, exists only in mentality, 22.

Fatalism, a superstition, 163; its view of the world, 165; not determinism, 106; not necessitarianism, 163, 164.

Fate of Romans not necessity, 164.

Father, God so called in Christian mythology, 49.

Fathers, their misunderstanding of parables, 196.

Faust, Goethe's, quoted, 147, 196, 208.

Feeling, common to all states of consciousness, 10; its definition, 189, 113; its relation to thought, 207; its various forms, 10, 190, 192; the heart of nature, 20; the subjective side of motion, 16.

Feeling substance, apperception its activity, 185.

Feelings arise from subjectivity, 17; cannot exist in isolation, 16, 182, 183, 191; their representative function, 11, 39, 191; units of soul-life, 16.

Fetish ideas compared with fetish images, 199.

Fetishism of atheists, 128; of dogmatists, 199; of the absolute, 128; the most primitive idolatry, 199.

Final causes, 144, 156.

Finitude demands special explanation, 93; of space involves antinomy, 96, 97.

First cause, a grotesque idea, 147; means ultimate reason, 146.

Flemming, his summation of Hegel's doctrine, 132.

Focussing of feelings in consciousness, 182, 183, 185, 191.

Folge opposed to *Grund*, 140.

Forces, not accounted for by mechanical laws, 162, 163; not causes, 139; spontaneous expressions of reality, 162.

Formal, its definition, 72, 78, 113; and sensory, the web and woof of knowledge, 35; called *a priori*, 61; distinguished from sensory by abstraction, 72; distinguished from material, 114; its function, 89; its necessity and universality, 113; its three degrees, 79, 86; Kant's views regarding it, 30, 31; same in mind as in things, 88; the condition of systematised experience, 78; the most important part of reality, 112.

Formal cause, defined by Aristotle, 143; cognition, considered empty by Kant, 35; combinations, part of existence in general, 72; laws, their relation to consciousness, 113, 130; magnitudes, created by mental acts, 60.

Formal sciences, enumerated, 110; explained by monism, 178; must be based on facts, 91; their function and value, 71, 78, 134; their nature, 35, 86, 115.

Formal thought, conditions of its evolution, 78; impossible to animals, 78; its practical value, 78, 107, 116.

Formal truths, not abstract generalisations, 61; not axioms nor intuitive principles, 61, 77.

Form, a property of all existence, 72, 88; as real as matter, 105; attributed to objects by mind, 87; objects always different in, 192; its changes not causation, 152; its changes the field of science, 42, 166; its laws universal, 105; not a cause, 144.

Forms make things what they are, 112; their perpetual flux, 130.

Forms of feeling, 10, 11, 192; of thought, 35, 60.

Fortnightly Review, cited, 95.

Fourfold root of principle of sufficient reason, 148.

Free actions immediate expressions of character, 160.

Freedom, illustrated by a magnet, 162, 163; its definition, 160; not limited to man, 161.

Free-will, analogous to spontaneity of nature, 162; compatible with necessity, 160, 164; its significance, 159.

French positivists, their fundamental principle, 69.

Fundamental problems disposed of, iii.

Fusion of ideas different from association, 175.

Future dependent on the ideal, 169; the best legacy to, 210; the present to be sacrificed to, 168.

Galton, Francis, invented composite photography, 178.

Gedankenwesen, a synonym of noumena, 133.

Gegenstand, coined to represent "object," 14.

General laws superseded by universal, 155.

General notion, God not such, 147.

General notions, empty, 146; explained by monism, 178; presupposed by particular ones, 182; the conditions of cognition, 181.

Generalisation, analogous to composite photography, 178; lowest faculty of mind, 182; not explained by association, 195; prior to cognition, 181; product of abstract thought, 194.

Generic images, their origin, 175.

Genesis, cited, 129.

Genius, result of work of ancestors, 171.

Geometrical figures, their value, 116; method, its fault, 90.

Geometry, a purely formal science, 79, 110, 111; its analogy with logic, 110; its presupposition, 55, 57, 111; its construction of space, 89, 93; non-Euclidean ones possible, 80, 81, 82, 109; not dependent on empiric space, 96.

German terminology adopted by other nations, 14; text-books, their definition of space, 92.

Glory of moral law, 202.

God, a moral idea, 147; an abstract idea, 19; concrete and real, 147; how revealed to man, 37, 201, 209; inconceivable unless triune, 101; not a big human being, 202; not a general notion, 147; not a great world-ego, 147; not immoral, 170; not the Absolute, 128, 129; not the author of creeds, 197; not the ultimate reason, 146; of dogmatist anthropomorphic, 202; of New Testament, 129; the all-existence in which we move, 49; the authority of conduct, 170; the Son distinguished from Father, 101; the Spirit, proceeds from Father and Son, 101; worship of his symbols idolatry, 199; worshipped because his commandments are true, 203.

God-Man, implies Trinity, 101.

Goethe, cited, 196.

Goltz, Professor, his psychological experiments, 180.

Gospels, their account of resurrection, 188; their teaching of self-sacrifice, 198; the Jesus of the, 196.

Grassmann, cited, 53-56, 92.

Gravitation, a form of will, 158, 164; not a law, but a formula, 164.

Gravity, not a cause, but a property, 138, 139, 140, 142, 164.

Greek, deity Moira not necessity, 164; poets their symbolisms, 197.

Growth, a property of cells, 168.

Grund distinguished from *Ursache*, 143; opposed to *Folge*, 140.

Hallucinations, real as sensations, 21.

Hamilton, Sir William, cited, 124, 125.

Happiness, not basis of ethics, 167; not increased by evolution, 6; not object of life, 197.

Harmony, of universe, 158, 177, 202; produced by character, 165; produced by formal laws, 130.

Hartley, his psychology of association, 173.

Hearing, its cerebral centre, 180.

Heat, its perception and abstraction, 127.

Heathenism, its essence, 197.

Hegel, on the absolute, 132; on the trinity-relation, 100.

Henism, name for one-substance theory, 3.

Hobbes, his psychology of association, 175.

Hindu, nations, causes of their downfall, 23; philosophies, their mystery, 21.

Historical elements of religion unessential, 196, 197; interest of the dogmatist, 200; investigation of resurrection, 188.

History of religions, 204.

Höffding, his psychology of association, 175.

Holiness of the religious ideal, 210.

Homoloidality of space, 95, 98, 111.

Hope, its importance, 167.

Human reason, reflection of world-reason, 117.

Humanity, its sacrifice, 167.

Hume, his influence upon Kant, 30; his psychology of association, 75, 175; his scepticism, 29, 151.

Huxley, Professor, his confusion of thought, 120, 121.

Hypotheses, not necessary to purely formal sciences, 111; of scientists, need not be accepted, 206.

Idea of God, not a myth nor an abstraction, 159; superstitiously regarded, 147.

Idea worshippers, their idolatry, 200, 203.

Ideal, of invisible church, 199; its relation to religion, 204, 209, 210; of Hindu subjectivism, 24; the guide of progress, 169; the struggle for the, 198.

Ideas, defined, 186, 192; always general, 118, 181, 182; communicated by symbols, 197; more empty when more general, 146; Platonic view of, 133; symbols of reality, 121, 134; the conditions of experience, 65; their association, 173, 174; their individuality, 187, 188; their life, 186; their migration, 187; their origin, 125, 178, 187; their power, 188; their relation to the will, 192; their rivalry, 187; true or untrue, 47; value of religious, 204.

INDEX.

Identity, the foundation of rational thought, 109, 113.
Idolatry, its definition, 200, 201; its cause, 200, 201; its essence, 197; its varieties, 202; of agnostics, 202, 203; of dogmatists, 200, 203, 207; of the Absolute, 128, 200.
Illusion, none in nature or sensation, 21, 22.
Illusoriness of reason to nominalists, 104.
Ill-will, its futility, 208.
Image, definition of, 90.
Image of God, the anthropomorphic, 202.
Images, their idolatrous worship, 199.
Imagination defined, 193.
Immanent teleology of nature, 158.
Immorality, disobedience to God, 170; of nature, an absurdity, 170.
Immortality of soul, 188, 189.
Impact necessary to objectivity, 15.
Impenetrability, Huxley's view of, 120.
Impressions, not received passively in apperception, 185.
Impulses, their definition, 192.
Independence, deficient in dogmatists, 200.
India illustrates fatal results of pessimism, 23.
Individuality of ideas, 188.
Indolence, causes idolatry, 200.
Induction, its problem in Mill's view, 114.
Inductive reason called *a posteriori*, 63.
Inexplicable, things not so, 177.
Infidels, 189.
Infinite, always tripartite, 100, 102; an absurd idea, 200; idolatry of, 201.
Infinite-dimensioned space possible, 94.
Infinitude, a matter of course, 93; a simpler conception than finitude, 97.
Infinity of homoloidal space not an antimony, 96.
Innate ideas, 28.
Innerness not the whole of reality, 25.
Inquiry, caused by doubt, 208; its aid to religion, 207.

Insight lacked by idea-worshippers, 200.
Inspiration, the source of knowledge to mystics, 26.
Intellect, its definition, 194.
Intellectual Powers, Reid's, quoted, 148.
Intelligence, its definition, 194.
Intelligent beings, their spontaneity called will, 184.
Intensification of feeling the function of consciousness, 182, 183, 191.
Interactions constitute reality, 18.
Interpretation of sensation sometimes erroneous, 22.
Interrelation of feelings, 72, 191.
Intuition, as viewed by mystics, 26; contrasted with abstract thought, 126; contrasted with self-observation, 61; furnishes data of sense-impression, 125; meaning of the word, 9; the great support of false doctrines, 69; the theory abandoned, 37; yields sensations, 127.
Inventions in formal sciences, 134.
Invisible church, its religion true, 199.
Irreligion, remedied by science, 208.
Isosceles triangle, demonstrated by Thales, 86.
Israelitic religion, its relation to moral truths, 27.

Jesus, established no dogmas, 206; his new kingdom, 106; his resurrection, 188, 189; spoke in parables, 196; would be rejected by churches, 198.
Judgment, its definition, 193, 194; its origin, 190.

Kant, cited, 9, 30–33, 56, 64, 65, 74, 77, 86, 88, 89, 133, 148; his apriorism reconciled with empiricism, iii; his mistakes, 31, 34, 36; his theory of knowledge, 26–29, 35, 66, 70, 86, 87, 177; his view of axioms, 59; his view of the ego, 68; secret of his greatness, 36; source of his transcendentalism, 113.
Kantism, its truths and errors both rejected by Mill, 70.

INDEX.   221

Kant's Critical Problem, cited, 74, Critique of Pure Reason, cited, iii.

Kiesewetter, Prof., his discussions with Kant, 33.

Kingdom of heaven, its true character, 49.

Kirchhoff, his definition of knowledge, 37.

Kismet, of Mohammedans, not necessity, 164.

Klein, his elliptical geometry, 80.

Knowledge, definitions of the word, 37, 39, 41; extended by formal schedules, 116; impossible in nominalist theory, 104; its acquisition the sphere of science, 40; its source, 26, 35, 38, 73, 76, 177, 178; not an association of single sensations, 114; purified by science, 42; rendered definite by naming, 39; the basis of all action, 39; the measure of mentality, 39; unnecessary to purely formal sciences, 111.

Kronos, a symbol of time, 197.

Labor of past generations not lost, 171.

Lambert, his definition of *a priori*, 64.

Language, its relation to thought, 107, 108, 123, 125, 186.

Law, identified by Lewes with causes, 149; its uniformity and universality, 50; of causation governs character, 166; of gravitation a descriptive formula, 164; of progression in logic, 56; of self-consistency of being, 112; of the ideal, 169.

Laws, based on universal and necessary truths, 76; of association, 173; of God, their blessings to be worked out, 202; of mechanics a revelation of spirit, 24; of nature, defined, 1, 48, 139, 140, 149, 155, a mystery to associationists, 177, immutable, 159, 202, not immoral, 170, require further explanation, 154; special, superseded by general, 155; their authority, 204; widely different from thoughts, 149.

Learned, their superstitions, 51.

Leibnitz, cited, 13, 29, 63.

Letter, easier to believe than spirit, 196.

Lewes, George Henry, his views of causation, 149, 150, 251.

Liberty compatible with necessity, 160.

Life, its true aims, 6, 197.

Light, a form of will, 184; its apprehension an act of abstraction, 107; path of its rays, 85, 97, 98, 99; the quickest motion known, 97.

Limits between provinces of reality purely ideal, 121.

Lindemann, Prof., cited, 80.

Line, its definition, 89; its properties, 95; new method for its production, 96.

Littré, his positivism really agnosticism, 2.

Lobatschewsky's space, 81.

Locke, cited, 28; his definition of cause, 149; his theory of knowledge, 29, 75.

Logarithms, 103.

Logic, impossibility of a new kind, 109; a rigidly formal science, 79, 110, 111; its analogy with geometry, 110; its nature, 35; laws of progress in, 56; might be considered a branch of astronomy, 44.

Logical categories, their nature, 116; consequence of a reason, 141; necessity, its mystery, 115; principles universal and necessary, 71.

Logicalness of confessions of faith, 196.

Logos, the word of truth, 49.

Love, should be the mainspring of action, 198, 199; the foundations of the new covenant, 206.

Lucretius, cited, 195.

Mach, Ernst, cited, 43.

Magnet, an illustration of freedom and compulsion, 162.

Magnitudes, their names should be constant, 61.

Man, creeds his work not God's, 197; his origin, 171; made divine by the truth, 205; not a mere mechanism,

INDEX.

165; thought his exclusive prerogative, 118, 123, 125, 134.

Mansel, cited, 124.

Material, cause, 143, 150; importance of distinguishing it from formal, 114; not a cause, 144; world is being as it appears, 23.

Materialism, its errors, 19; its view of the universe, 129; not true monism, 3.

Mathematical, operations take place in space, 92; space and abstraction not construction, 101; symbols to be regarded as words, 39.

Mathematicians, do not distinguish degrees of formal, 83; their recent theories about space, 95; their superstitions, 51.

Mathematics, its nature, 35, 91, 116; certitude of its principles, 71, 131; divinity in, 207; its data the results of abstraction, 101; its demonstrations compared with chemical analysis, 74; its presuppositions, 56, 91, 92; Kant's view of its truths, 29, 59; not a mere fiction, 134; not so *a priori* as arithmetic, 80; Schopenhauer's view of its certitude, 53, 55; the model science, 51; various kinds invented, 109.

Matter, an abstract idea, 4, 19; an appearance of existence, 21; a quality, not an entity, 122; in motion a true picture of the world, 21; its conservation implies causation, 135; its form and composition changeable, 166; its motions a revelation of soul, 22; its persistence, 159; its relation to the unconditioned, 130; its total amount constant, 42, 166; not energy, 121; not the explanation of soul, 111; an element of objectivity, 12, 14; transformed in causation, 152.

Matthew, St., cited, 50.

Maxims not the basis of investigations, 58.

Meaning of feelings, 11.

Meanings, of structures the condition of apperception, 185; of words constitute ideas, 186.

Mechanical, explanation of nature inadmissible, 161, 162; laws, their function and value, 162; not antispiritual, 24; phenomena compared with compulsion, 161.

Mechanics, its laws a revelation of spiritual activity, 24; not so *a priori* as algebra, 80.

Mechanism, of nature only an appearance, 20; of nature and man not dead, 165.

Medicine-man, his spells, 202.

Meliorism, the true and the false, 5, 6, 167.

Memory, its definition, 190, 193; essential to consciousness, 183; the condition of experience, 26.

Memory-images, 174, 179, 190.

Memory-structures, the basis of psychic life, 184; the condition of apperception, 185; their function, 180, 181, 182, 192.

Mental, conditions of apperception, 185; life, its debt to nature, 186.

Mental operations, their nature, 60, 111; depend on internal experience, 61; presupposed by mathematics, 92; the germ of reason, 117; their elements, 116; the only material of pure mathematics, 116.

Mentality, dependent on knowledge, 39.

Mephistopheles, quoted, 196.

Mercury, as a "cause" of death, 150, 151.

Messiahship of Jesus, 206.

Metaphysical, character attributed to the *a priori*, 68; conception of God erroneous, 146; noumena not, 133; speculations, to be abandoned, 4.

Methods, of philosophy, 51; of science should be adopted by religion, 209; of scientific work, 42; of thought, 118; the subject of philosophical study, 45.

Microscopy and mathematics. 116.

Middle Ages, philosophical parties in, 103.

Mill, John, his psychology of association, 173.

Mill, John Stuart, his empiricism reconciled with apriorism, iii; his mistakes, 70, 75, 114, 173; his view of the *a priori*, 59, 68, 69, 75.

Milton, cited, 108.

Mind, its definition, 192, 193; a necessary outcome of living, 20; generalisation its lowest faculty, 182; its origin, 22, 25, 178; its universal activity, 88; its yearning for truth, 50; no breach between it and nature, 20. 88, 112, 181; the basis of formal sciences, 91.

Model of reality constructed in mind, 89.

Modern idolatry worse than that of savages, 199.

Mohammedan Kismet, not necessity, 164.

Moira of Greeks not necessity, 164.

Monism, its definition, 3, 19, 50; appreciates both spirit and matter, 23; avoid errors of Kant and associationists, 177; can alone give peace, 50; corroborated by the advance of science, 4; derived from dualism through triunism, 101; dominates modern thought, 1; not a finished system, 4; not understood by its opponents, 3; not the one-substance theory, 3; of Brahmans, its one-sidedness and fatal results, 23.

Monist, The, cited, 24, 84, 132, 161.

Monistic character of necessitarianism, 165; positivism not a new philosophy, 4.

Moon, measurement of its distance *a priori*, 106.

Moral aspiration, of churches, 198; same as natural living, 171.

Moral endeavor, not a matter of choice, 167.

Moral idea of God, 147; ideas, their power, 188.

Moral, laws true and useful, 201-203; tendency the fundamental law of nature, 169; truths, a natural growth, 27; world-order, its harmony, 202; worth, how estimated, 163.

Morality, its nature, 7, 168, 170; agrees with constitution of universe, 170; dependent on necessity, 163; its basis, 198; of traditional religions, correct, 170, 198; of true religion, 199; the means of evolution, 171.

Motions, an element of objectivity, 12, 14, 15; governed by mechanical laws, 162; never aimless, 157; primary and scondary constitute phenomena, 161; that of light quickest known, 97; the experience of existence, 51; the objective side of feeling, 16; the world composed of, 111.

Motiv, Schopenhauer's use of the term, 148.

Motor ideas, 186.

Müller, Max, cited, 107, 108.

Multi-dimensional bodies, their possibility, 92.

Muscular sense, its function an abstraction, 127.

Mysteries in philosophy, 146; in religion, 27, 29.

Mysteriousness, of cognition denied, 181; of things denied, 177.

Mystery, in natural law to associationists, 175, 177; of logical necessity, 115.

Mysticism, avoided by monism, 177; in Kantian apriorism, 36, 66, 67, 71; introduced into mathematics by Schopenhauer, 55; the outcome of associationism, 177.

Mystics, their view of the source of knowledge, 26.

Mythological idea of God not prevalent, 147.

Mythology of Christianity unimportant, 198.

Names, their function in thought, 39, 123, 124.

Natura naturans, 101; *naturata*, 101.

Natural laws, their nature, 1, 130, 139, 140, 148; a mystery to associationists, 177; require explanation, 152.

Natural living identical with moral aspiration, 171.

Natural processes, analogous to mental operations, 111; not explainable mechanically, 161.

Nature, a revelation of God, 21, 22, 26, 209; aspiration the grandest of its tendencies, 171; its character, 164, 165; its harmony and order, 158; its laws the written will of God, 201; its operations identical with those of mind, 88; its order recognised by religious leaders, 170; its spontaneity analogous to will, 161, 162, 165, 184; its unchangeableness, 159, 202; its universal activity, 88; necessity not a power above it, 164; no break in, 181; not a dead mechanism, 165; not immoral, 170; of things, 161, 166; obedience to it the true worship, 201; the grand apocalypse, 26, 205; the ideal its law, 169.

Necessary truths, denied by Mill, 70; in logic and mathematics, 71.

Necessitarianism, distinguished from fatalism, 165; the foundation of science, 163.

Necessity, its definition, 160, 161; compatible with free will, 160, 164; denied by association philosophy, 177; distinguished from compulsion, 160; implied by causation, 160; its problem same as that of universality, 105; logical, its mystery, 115; not compulsion, 106, 164; not Moira, Fate or Kismet, 164; of formal truths, 75, 76, 108, 175; of teleology in nature, 158.

Nervous system, its function in feeling, 183.

New covenant made by Jesus, 206; Testament, its view of God. 129.

Newton, his misuse of the word axiom, 52.

Noiré, cited, 107, 108.

Nominalism, described, 103; a reaction against errors of realism, 71; cannot explain construction of triangles, 107; less true than realism, 70, 108, 174; not free from assumptions, 105; the source of agnosticism, 104; the source of sensationalism, 177.

Nominalistic controversy, forgotten, 124; its outcome, 122.

Non-Euclidean geometry, its possibility, 80–83, 109; space, its possibility, 90, 92.

Norm, of aspiration, 204; of thought 194.

Nose, its function an abstraction 127.

Notions, derived from reality, 117; general and particular, 182.

Noumena, their nature, 122, 133, 134, 148.

Numbers, their nature and origin, 34, 78.

Obedience to God, 147, 170, 203.

Object and subject inseparable, 14.

Objective, its definition, 13, 14; existence disparaged by Hindu philosophers, 21; experience necessary to knowledge, 25; formal and material inseparable in the, 36.

Objectivism, a synonym for materialism, 20.

Objectivity, its definition, 12, 16, 17, 21; an abstraction, 17; appears as matter moving in space, 12, 14, 15; furnishes means of experience, 25; history of the term, 12–14; of form and relation, 72; of nature a revelation, 21, 22, 26; of reason, 117, 175; of relations, 103; of truth, 48.

Objects, always different in form, 191; Kant's view of, 86, 87; of this work, iii; their real nature, 14, 15, 16, 46; their representation in feeling, 11, 15.

Observation, a function of science, 153.

Old religions, compared with agnosticism, 203; not to be destroyed, 209.

One-substance theory properly called henism, 3.

Ontological school, its vice, 90.

Optimism, its definition, 6; meliorism not a modification of, 5.

Order of the universe, its cause, 158, 159; denied by association-philosophy, 177.

Organ of cognition in Kant's system, 66.

Organisation and systematisation of feeling, 183.

Organism, its relation to apperception, 185; social, 168.

INDEX.

Organisms, governed by ethical principle, 169.

Orthodox conception of resurrection materialistic, 189.

Orthodoxy, the religion of science, 209.

Outerness not all of reality, 25.

Oxygen, its chemical effect on amœba, 186.

Pagan, elements in religion, 39, 220; view of the resurrection, 189.

Paganism, among atheists, 128; being eliminated from Christianity, 199; considers abstracts real essences, 133; its essence, 197; its fatalism, 164; of dogmatists, 199, 200, 203.

Pain, volition increases sensitiveness to, 6.

Particular notions subsequent to general, 181, 182.

Parables, are vehicles of truth, 196; taken literally by church Christians, 196; to be understood allegorically, 203.

Parallaxes of stars, their measurement, 83.

Parallels, axiom of, 95, 110.

Passions exactly defined, 192.

Path of a ray of light the prototype of straight lines, 97.

Percept, its definition, 190.

Perception, cognition a form of, 194; different from sensation, 180; its exact definition, 190; its physiological process, 182; Kant's definition of, 33; the beginning of apperception, 182; the simplest act of cognition, 38, 181, 186.

Perceptions, their nature, 48, 179, 181.

Peirce, Charles S., cited, 24.

Peripatetic philosophy, its theory of knowledge, 28.

Peripheral angles of a circle, their equality, 84.

Person, its definition, 191.

Personality, its nature, 184, 188; of ideas, 188.

Pessimism, 6, 23.

Phenomena, a synonym for atsights, 133; their nature, 148; their primary and secondary motions, 161; their relation to noumena, 134.

Philology, its explanation of reason, 107.

Philosophasters, in the majority, 36.

Philosophers, should also be scientists, 46; their ancient mistakes, 133; their greatest difficulty, 118, 119; worship their own errors, 146.

Philosophical background, needed by science, 14; idea of God not prevalent, 147; parties of the Middle Ages, 103.

Philosophical, Letters of Schiller, cited, 207; Review, cited, 74.

Philosophy, its definition, 4, 45, 90, 146; association not its fundamental principle, 175; axioms inadmissible in, 58; based upon experience, 9, 37, 51; ignored by scientists, iv; its most fundamental problem, 2, 73; its quarrels over final causes, 156; its recent decline, iv; its relation to progress, iv; its usefulness, iv, 4, 207; its wildcat banks, 135; injured by use of the term absolute, 127; of association criticised, 173; solves problems of experience, 137; tested by its ethics, 5; the ontological school of, 90.

Phosphorus, its properties an illustration of character, 165.

Photographs, composite, illlustrate generalisation, 178.

Physics, its field of inquiry, 43, 44.

Physiological process of perception, 182.

Piano, an illustration of causation, 137, 142.

Plane geometry, 57, 83, 89.

Plane, non-Euclidean, possible, 58.

Planets, evolution on other, 168, 171.

Plato, his view of ideas, 133.

Poets of Greece, their symbolisms, 197.

Point, criticism of its former definition, 91, 92; not a real object, 92; used for construction of space, 89, 93.

Point of view of this work, iii.

Political songs of England, quoted, 79

Polygonal relations reducible to triple relations, 100.
Popular usage usually accurate, 143.
Positive monism not new, 4.
Positivism, 1, 2, 45, 69.
Postulates of Euclid, 52, 58, 60.
Practical, ends sought by science, 42; life, religion relates to, 207; view of God as authority, 147.
Practicalness of decalogue, 202.
Prayer, only a self-discipline, 202; should not be precatory, 200, 202.
Preacher, usefulness of positive philosophy to, 4.
Presence of Christ in humanity, 189.
Priests, not the true prophets of religion, 205.
Primer of Philosophy, its meaning and object, iii.
Primum appellatum, 181.
Primum cognitum, 181.
Principles, not the basis of investigation, 58; never self-evident, 148; of mathematics, Kant's view of, 59.
Problem, of universality, necessity, and reason, 105, 106; the most fundamental in philosophy, 73.
Problems, (Lewes's,) cited, 149; fundamental, disposed of, iii; not all solved, 4.
Progress, fatal to dogmatism, 210; formerly led by philosophy, iv; guided by the ideal, 169; its conditions, 167, 189, 200, 204; its relation to happiness, 6; opposed by false Christianity, 196; scientific, corroborates monism, 4.
Progression, law of, in mathematics and logic, 56.
Prolegomena Logica, cited, 124.
Propagation, a property of cells, 168.
Protozoa, their exhibition of will, 185, 186; their tendencies not different from chemical affinities, 186.
Pseudopods of amœba, their explanation, 186.
Pseudo-reason impossible, 110.
Psychical, its definition, 192; conditions of apperception, 185; life based on memory, 189; the heart of nature, 20.

Psychological, mistakes of association philosophy, 175; terms, their definition, 189.
Psychology, its domain, 43, 122; its function, 44; its laws, 173; of association, its teachers, 175.
Purely formal, its function, 89; its distinction from rigidly formal overlooked by Kant, 86.
Purely formal sciences, 79, 110, 111.
Pure reason, its nature, 91, 112, 117; discredited by Comte, 68; its agreement with configurations of reality, 107, 112.
Purpose, its definition, 157, 192; consecration to, 204; essential to will, 186; its relation to causality, 144.
Pythagorean theorem, Schopenhauer's view of it, 53.

Qualities, causative, in the cause, 140; rational, in actions, 166.

Raison d'être, distinguished from cause, 143.
Rational inquiry into truth always necessary, 207.
Rational thought, its identity with abstract thought, 123; its limit the beginning of idolatry, 201.
Rationality of decalogue, 202.
Ratio, distinguished from cause, 143.
Ratio sui, its real meaning, 145.
Rays of light, their nature, 98; their path, 85, 97.
Reaction of chemicals a form of will, 184.
Realism, described, 103; its extravagances, 70; *versus* nominalism, 71, 108, 124, 174.
Reality, its nature, 12, 18, 20, 105; as conceived by two philosophical parties, 103, 104; contains both subject and object, 14; has features determinable by pure reason, 107, 112; how revealed to reason, 108; independent of thought, 88, 89; its difference from truth, 46, 47; its reaction necessary to development of mind, 25; its universally necessary features, 70; its ultimate springs, 162; its unity, 119, 121; of law of

INDEX.

sameness in nature, 112; of the ideal, 169; symbolised in abstracts, 118, 121, 134; the same everywhere, 155; the source of notion, 117; truly represented to senses, 21.

Reason, its nature, iii, 107, 109, 111, 118, 194, 195; always consistent, 110; dependent on formal knowledge, 77; distinguished from understanding, 30; implies realism, 104; its aid to religion, 207; its authority, 175; its function, 117, 118; its necessity, 175; its norm, 108; its origin, 108, 112, 116, 117; its possibility, 76; its problem that of determinability,106; its unity, 108, 109; not explained by association, 175; not purely subjective, 117, 175; scorned by priests, 205; source of its credibility, 108; the method of experience, 117; ultimate, the source of other reasons, 146; universal in its nature, 109.

Reasoning, formal, as viewed by Kant, 30; its processes, 60, 64, 91.

Reasons, correlative with consequences, 140; distinguished from causes, 139; the object of scientific research, 154.

Recollection, motor-ideas dependent on, 186.

Reconciliation of rival philosophies, iii.

Reflection, source of notions of causation, 148.

Reid, his view of causation, 148.

Relations always triune, 18, 100, 101.

Religio-philosophical convictions, their importance, 23.

Religion, its nature, 205, 207; explained by positive philosophy, 5; identified with Christianity, 196, 199; inseparable from science, 204, 205, 207; its basis, 178, 189, 205; needs enthusiasm and zeal, 209; not identical with science,207; of invisible church that of science, 199; only one true one, 205; priests not always its prophets, 205; science the basis of its progress, 204; supernaturalism, a pagan element of, 37; the basis of conduct, 204.

Religion of science, its nature, 203, 210; discards duality of truth, 205; not meant to destroy old ones, 209; the highest ideal, 209; the revelation of moral laws, 202.

Religions, their common ideal, 209; their history, 204; their morality correct, 170.

Religious, duty of the scientist, 206; evolution of mankind, 200; ideal, the true and holy, 210; sentiments, their power, 188; teachers of mankind, 169, 170.

Representations, the contents of states of consciousness, 11.

Resistance and extension, Huxley's view of, 120.

Resurrection, its profound truth, 189; pagan view of, 188.

Revelation, its true method, 37; in nature, 21, 199, 209; of God in truth, 49; of moral laws through science, 202; supernatural, 27, 37; tradition as considered, 205.

Riemann's space, 80, 81, 92, 94, 109.

Right exists only in mentality, 22.

Rigidly formal, its function, 88, 89; always reliable in experience, 111; character of reason, 111; not distinguished by Kant, 86; sciences, 39, 110, 111.

Robertson, Prof. G. C., on axioms, 60.

Roman Fate, not necessity, 164.

Rotation applied to geometrical production of lines, 97, 99.

Rules of reasoning, 58, 60.

Sacredness of truths of science, 209.

Sacrifice, its importance, 167, 168, 198, 199.

Salvation not dependent on dogmas, 196.

Sameness of nature, 109, 111, 112, 113.

Sanctity of moral law, 202.

Savages, average public compared to, 135; their idolatry compared with modern kind, 199.

Saviour, implies Trinity, 101.

Scepticism, of Hume, its source, 152; the outcome of associationism, 177; the root of nominalism, 104.

Schiller, cited, 45, 207.

Scholastic philosophy, terms invented by, 62; theorem on causality, 150, 152.

Schopenhauer, his suggestion for improvement of mathematical method, 54, 55; his view of *a priori*, 59; his view of causation, 147, 148; his view of will, 184, 185; on Euclidean demonstration, 53.

Schurmann, Prof. J. G., cited, 74, 75.

Science, its nature, 41,145, 205; a revelation of moral laws, 202; beginning to enlighten churches, 198; corroborates gospel, 198; corroborates monism, 4; full of superstitions, 51; its aim, 40, 43; its basis, 37, 43, 76; its relation to religion, 205, 207; its faith in causation, 156; its function, 42, 153; its history, 209; its holiness, 206, 209; its methods, 42, 43, 78; its need of a philosophic background, iv; its production of religious progress, 204; proves immortality of soul, 189; the basis of civilisation, 204; the chief means of progress, 206.

Sciences, formal, their superiority, 115; their relations studied by philosophy, 45; their provinces artificially established by abstraction, 43, 44.

Scientific, certainty, 144; discoveries, 5; inquiry, 45, 170, 178.

Scientists, should be philosophers, iv, 46; their supposed vagaries, 205.

Sects, their future, 209, 210.

Seelentaub, meaning of the expression, 180.

Self-consistency of being, its law, 112.

Self-discipline, prayer only a, 202.

Self-evident principles do not exist, 148.

Self-observation, a form of experience, 61.

Self-sacrifice the path to victory, 198.

Sensation, its definition, 180, 189.

Sensationalism, derived from nominalism, 177; the basis of positivism, 69.

Sensations, always real, 47, 48; always trustworthy, 21, 22, 39; analysed by abstraction, 126, 127; constitute experience, 113; how transformed into feeling, 183; not felt when isolated, 191; not the source of notion of causation, 148; our *Anschauung*, 126; their cause, 11; their relation to cognition, 31, 33, 180,181, 182; their significance, 11, 105; the material of mind, 72, 77, 190.

Sense-experience, always reliable,22; considered blind by Kant, 35; not able to establish a universal relation, 113; the basis of abstract ideas, 126.

Sense-illusion, never occurs, 22.

Sense-impressions, always systematically connected, 71, 72; contains a formal element, 34, 72; how connected according to Kant, 66; interpreted by memory-structures, 181; signs of things, 179; the data of experience, 74; their data furnished by intuition, 125; their registry, 179; their selection in evolution, 185.

Sensory,and formal,the web and woof of knowledge, 35; contrasted with formal, 72; phenomena, their irregularity, 113.

Sentiency of memory-structures the condition of apperception, 185.

Sentient symbols defined, 192.

Sentiment defined, 190.

Seinsgrund, Schopenhauer's use of term, 148.

Separations and combinations compose nature, 111.

Sequence, distinguished from consequence, 141; not the whole of causation, 176.

Similarity, association of ideas by, 173, 174.

Sinneswesen, a synonym of phenomena, 133.

Sirius, used as an illustration, 92, 93.

Skin, its function an abstraction, 127.

Smell, 127, 190.

Society dependent on moral laws, 201.

Solids, their geometrical construction, 90.

Son of God, the word of truth, 49.

INDEX.

Sound, its perception an act of abstraction, 127; symbols, their relation to soul-life, 186.

Soul, its nature, 4, 19, 25, 119, 188, 192, 193; inseparable from body, 23; its elements, 179; its immortality, 188, 189; its importance, 24; its unity denied by Kant, 68; kingdom of heaven in the, 49; not in all things, 16; not knowable without objective experience, 25; sensations its atoms, 190.

Soul-blindness, 180.

Soul-life, apperceptions its acts, 186.

Souls, of things known through notions of matter, 22; power of ideas over, 188.

Space, its nature, 21, 92, 93, 111, 122; an element of objectivity, 12, 14, 15; defects of old method of its construction, 91; its infinity, 94; its various kinds, 81, 90, 93, 109; mathematical, an abstraction not a construction, 101; presupposed by mathematics, 56, 80, 91, 92; problem of its homoloidality, 84, 96, 98; problem of its three dimensions, 89, 99; the pure form of the world, 111.

Space-conceptions not properly axioms, 56.

Space-relations, homoloidality a method of computing, 96.

Spatial relations, no insight of them obtainable from Euclid, 53.

Special laws superseded by general, 155.

Spencer, Herbert, cited, 120, 175.

Speech, creates rational thought, 186.

Spells, prayer compared with, 202.

Spinoza, his theory of knowledge, 28; his view of causation, 145.

Spirit, its definition, 193; an abstract idea, 4, 19; its activity revealed in mechanics, 24; more difficult to understand than letter, 196; of God, distinguished from Father and Son, 101.

Spiritual, its definition, 192.

Spiritualism, its errors, 19; not true monism, 3.

Spirituality of all existence, 20.

Spontaneity, defined, 101; of intelligent beings called will, 184; of nature, 161, 162, 165, 184; of primitive apperception, 185.

Spontaneous motion of things, 162.

Spring of cosmic life, 172.

Star of Bethlehem, ethical principle compared to, 169.

States of consciousness, their elements, 10.

Stereometry a purely formal science, 79.

Stone, its action in falling spontaneous, 164.

Straight line, its definitions and properties, 89, 90, 95-98.

Straightness, difficulty of defining it, 90, 96; not a quality of space, 95; not demonstrable by moving point, 89.

Subject and object inseparable, 14.

Subjective, existence objective to other subjects, 16; experience, limits of its functions, 25; reason a product of the world-order, 117.

Subjectivism, a synonym for idealism, 17.

Subjectivity, an abstraction, 17; attributed to relations by nominalists, 103; a universal feature of existence, 17; curious change in its meaning, 12-14, 17; formal and material inseparable in, 36; its relation to objectivity, 17, 21; of truth, 48; sensations its ultimate units, 190; the condition of experience, 25.

Substance, its persistence, 152, 159; not a cause, 144.

Subsumption, the beginning of cognition, 182.

Subtraction, scholastic use of term, 123.

Succession, causation more than, 151, 152.

Sufficient reason, Schopenhauer's use of term, 148.

Sully, cited, 124, 125.

Sun, measurement of its distance an *a priori* determination, 106.

Superindividual facts, their existence, 188.

Supernaturalism, an erroneous interpretation of experience, 37; its view of source of knowledge, 26, 27; to be abandoned, 4.

Superstition, found even among learned, 51; in certain kinds of prayer, 202; in fatalism, 163; religion of science free from, 209; religions transformed into, 205.

Suppression of search for truth, 205.

Sursum, the watchword of evolution, 171.

Syllogism, axiom of parallels analogous to, 110; presents a triad relation, 102.

Symbolic function, of ideas, 134; of adoration, 202.

Symbols, all words are, 197; Christian, true in meaning, 198; dogmatism their idolatry, 202; their worship idolatrous, 199.

System, its meaning, 40.

System of Logic (Mill's), cited, 114.

Systematising and organisation of feelings, 183.

Tabula rasa, mind compared with, by Locke, 28.

Talents, their origin, 171.

Taste, 127, 190.

Teachers of mankind, their insight into nature, 169, 170.

Teleology, problem of, 156, 158.

Temperature, nature of its perception, 127, 190.

Temporality demands special explanation, 94.

Tendency distinguished from will, 186, 187.

Terminology of psychology, 189.

Terms, old better than new, 159.

Thales, his demonstration of properties of triangle, 86.

Theorems of mathematics made axiomatic by Schopenhauer, 55.

Thingishness, 12, 14.

Things-in-themselves, non-existent, 122, 131.

Thomas Aquinas, his definition of truth, 46.

Thought, its nature, 73-77, 111, 125, 192; its criterion, 174; its importance, 24; its method, 118; its origin, 108; its relation to feeling, 207.

Time, its nature, 122; symbolised as Kronos, 197.

Tongue, its function an abstraction, 127; Totality of being, a unity, 121, 130; a reality, 129.

Touch, its images, 190.

Traces, defined, 190.

Tradition, its conservatism, 200; made the foundation of religion, 204, 205.

Traditional morality correct, 170.

Transformation, a universal law, 156; its nature, 155, 157; its order, 194; reveals causation, 151, 153, 155, 156; the object of scientific research, 154.

Transcendent, distinguished from transcendental, 67.

Transcendental idealism of Kant, 66, 87, 113.

Transcendentalism, to be abandoned, 4; unfortunate influence of word, 66.

Triangle, its geometrical properties, 83-85, 106, 107; in the nature of things, 100; used as an illustration, 113, 141.

Tridimensionality of space, an algebraic problem, 99; its arbitrariness, 93, 102; knowable only by experience, 82, 111.

Trinity, characteristic of all relations, 18, 100, 101; must be attributed to God, 101.

Triunism, identical with monism, 101.

Truth, its nature, 22, 46; always needs to be proved, 52; both subjective and objective, 48; distinguished from correctness, 49; distinguished from reality, 46, 47; importance of its search, 205, 207; its attributes; 3, 49, 50, 205, 206, 207; its criterion, 3, 50; its suppression a lie, 205, more powerful than error, 209; not dual, 205; of Gospel confirmed by science, 198; only predicable of mental relations, 46; originates together with mind, 48; parables its vehicle, 196; science the search for

it, 41, 42; should welcome criticism, 208; the basis of religion, 205; the fulfilment of mind, 50; the revelation of God, 49.
Truths, of reason the cement of knowledge, 76; of science, their sacredness, 209; their varying dignity, 47.
Truthfulness the condition of all religion, 210.
Twelfth axiom of Euclid, 57, 58.

Ueber die vierfache Wurzel des Satzes vom zureichenden Grund, cited, 148.
Uebersichtlich, defined, 40.
Uebersichtlichkeit, lacking in certain mathematical demonstrations, 54.
Ultimate Effect, prayer to the, 147.
Ultimate reason, 146.
Unconditioned, the, 128-130.
Understanding, defined, 194; distinguished from reason by Kant, 30; its supposed pre-existence, 33.
Uniformities of universe, 114, 177.
Unity, absolute, would be non-existence, 101; of reality, 119, 121; of soul a fallacy, 68; tendency of living beings to higher, 168.
Universal truths, 70, 71, 89.
Universality, a fact of experience, 105, 108; its problem same as that of necessity, 105; justification of its assumption, 104; of formal truths, 75, 76, 104; the problem of reason, 106.
Universals, as viewed by different philosophies, 103.
Universe, as viewed by different philosophies, 103; governed by mechanical laws, 158; has no universal key, 147; its laws unchangeable, 202; its order, 159, 176; not absolute, 129; the source of its life, 172.
Unknowable, does not exist, 177, 200; idolatry of the, 200, 202; origin of the conception, 36; the outcome of confusion of mind, 120; the supposed haven of philosophy, iv.
Unknown reached through necessary truths, 70.
Unmorality of nature, 170.

Unrelated, not predicable of any form of existence, 129.
Ursache, distinguished from *Grund*, 143; opposed to *Wirkung*, 140; Schopenhauer's use of term, 148.

Verités de raison, 75.
Verworn, Prof. Max, cited, 186.
Vices and virtues, their effects, 27 their resemblance, 165.
Victory, obtained through self-sacrifice, 198.
Vision, its cerebral centre, 180.
Visionary knowledge rejected, 37.
Visions all mistakes, 26.
Visual images, 190.

Welt als Wille und Vorstellung, cited, 53.
Will, its definition, 161, 162, 184, 192; caused by image of end to be obtained, 184, 185; displayed by protozoöns, 185; distinguished from tendency, 186, 187; how developed, 185; its relation to apperception, 184, 185; never acts without a motive or aim, 186; of God, 161, 162, 201, 202; of things, 161; spontaneity of nature its simplest form, 161, 184.
Wirklichkeit, explanation of term, 18.
Wirkung, opposed to *Ursache*, 140.
Wisdom, symbolised by Athene, 197.
Wolf, cited, 63.
Words, their function, 39; their symbolic character, 186, 197; used correctly by the masses, 143.
Works, their value, 171.
World, an abstract idea, 4, 19; an appearance but a revelation, 25; explainable whenever its wants are transformations, 156; governed by same laws as thought, 112; pictured truly to senses, 21; reason for its existence unknown, 93.
World-conception, evils of a false, 23; implied in gravitation, 164; to be based on verifiable facts, 2.
World-ego, God not a, 147,
World-flight, 23, 24.
World-order, 117.

World-reason, human reason its reflection, 117.
Worship, of error by philosophers, 146, 201; sectarian, its pagan features, 210; true, 201.
Wright, Tom, quoted, 29.
Wrong exists only in mentality, 22.

Yearning for truth the deepest impulse of mind, 50.

Zero, the absolute, 131.
Zoölogy, its field of inquiry, 43.
Zweckmässigkeit of nature, 158.

BOOKS AND ESSAYS ON KINDRED TOPICS BY THE SAME AUTHOR.

PHILOSOPHY.

FUNDAMENTAL PROBLEMS. Second edition. Pages, 373. Cloth, $1.50; Paper, 50 cts.—Contains discussions of the basic problems of philosophy, such as Ontology and Positivism; The Foundation of Monism; Form and Formal Thought; Metaphysics, the Use and Meaning of the Word; The Problem of Causality; Is Nature Alive? God as the Moral Law; Agnosticism and Positivism; Causation and Free Will; The Importance of Art.—The Appendix contains a number of replies to various critics, among which may be noted a series of controversies on Agnosticism (The Relativity of Knowledge, The Insolvable Problem, The Agnosticism of Modesty, etc.). A discussion on divine reason entitled The Sin Against the Holy Ghost. The Error of Materialism, In Reply to a Materialist.

OUR NEED OF PHILOSOPHY. An Appeal to the American People. An Address Delivered Before the World's Congress of Philosophy at Chicago, Ill.—Pages 14. Price, 5 cents.

THE PHILOSOPHY OF THE TOOL. A Lecture Delivered Before the Department of Manual and Art Education of the World's Congress Auxiliary.—Pages, 25. Price, 10 cents.

THE NATURE OF THE STATE. Contains the following chapters: Does the State Exist? Was the Individual Prior to Society? The State a Product of Natural Growth; The Modern State ; The Authority of the State and the Right to Revolution ; The Modern State Based Upon Revolution ; Treason and Reform.—Pages, 56. Price, 15 cents.

ARTICLES.

THE CRITERION OF TRUTH. Inquires into the Problem, What is Possible? It shows that "men who have the same world-conception will also have the same criterion of truth.' The main difficulty lies in distinguishing between facts and our interpretation of facts.—*The Monist*, Vol. I., No. 2. Page 229.

THE CONTINUITY OF EVOLUTION. The Science of Language Versus the Science of Life, as Represented by Prof. F. Max Müller and Prof. George John Romanes. Prof. F. Max Müller finds a gap in the evolution of life at the origin of man which renders the origin of language mysterious. The present article insists on the essential differences between man and animal but refuses to acknowledge that this constitutes a gap in nature, discussing both the idea of a creator as the God who moulds the world in its development, an argument in favor of continuous evolution.—*The Monist*, Vol. II., No. 1, page 70.

THE ORIGIN OF THOUGHT FORMS. I. Thought Forms and the Forms of Existence. II. The Problem of Apriority. III. The Conservation of Matter and Energy and Causation. IV. Why Is Mr. Mill's Proposition Untenable. V. The Meaning of "Necessary." VI. Modern Logic.—*The Monist*, Vol. II., No. 1, page 111.

COMTEAN POSITIVISM. (A review of Hermann Gruber's book.) The positivism of Comte and Littré was practically an agnosticism. The positivism upheld in *The Monist* and in

Dr. Carus's books is a new positivism which is a positivism in the true meaning of the word.—*The Monist*, Vol. II., No. 1, page 133. The same subject is treated in a controversy with Louis Belrose, Jr., *The Monist*, Vol. II., No. 3, pages 410–417, under the title Emile Littré's Positivism.

ARE THERE THINGS-IN-THEMSELVES? I. Things-In-Themselves and Noumena. II. Kant's View of Space and Time. III. Form Not Imported by the Mind Into Reality. IV. Professor Jodl's View of the Thing-in-Itself. V. Clifford's and Schopenhauer's Conceptions of the Thing-in-Itself. VI. Things and Relations. VII. Is the Ego a Thing-in-Itself? VIII. The Ego-Centric View Abandoned. IX. Personality and Evolution. X. Professor Mach's Position. XI. Truth in Mythology. XII. The Oneness of Subjectivity and Objectivity.—*The Monist*, Vol. II., No. 2, page 225.

THE DOCTRINE OF NECESSITY. A controversy with Charles S. Peirce. I. Mr. Charles S. Peirce's Onslaught on the Doctrine of Necessity (David Hume Redivivus). II. Causation Not Mere Sequence. III. Mr. Peirce's Logic of Science. IV. Necessity in Thought Presupposes Necessity in Facts. V. Mr. Peirce's Idea of the Evolution of Law. VI. World-Constructions. VII. Facts and Laws. VIII. Laws Not Inexplicable. IX. Conclusion.—*The Monist*, Vol. II., No. 4, page 560.

KANT AND SPENCER. (1) The Ethics of Kant. (2) Kant on Evolution. (3) Mr. Spencer on the Ethics of Kant.—*The Monist*, Appendix to Vol. II., No. 4, page 512. A letter from Mr. Spencer appears in *The Monist*, Vol. III., No. 2, page 272.

THE IDEA OF NECESSITY, ITS BASIS AND ITS SCOPE. I. The Basis of Necessity (The Idea of Sameness; Sameness and Mind; Samenesses a Fact; Eindeutig Bestimmt). II. The Scope of Necessity (Necessity and Chance; Free Will; Mechanical Philosophy; Spontaneity). Conclusion.—*The Monist*, Vol. III., No. 1, page 68.

THE FOUNDER OF TYCHISM, HIS METHODS, PHILOSOPHY, AND CRITICISMS. In Reply to Mr. Charles S. Peirce's Criticism. I. Differences of Method (Attention to Detail; Originality; A Modern Procrustes; Occam's Razor; The Application of Learning; The Principle of Positivism; Lopping Off the Absolute; The Theory of Probable Inference; Zweideutig Bestimmt; Explanation). II. Mr. Peirce's Philosophy (Duns Scotus, Mr. Peirce's Patron Saint; Mr. Peirce's Cosmogony; Tychism Unsatisfactory; The Negative Argument a Logical Fallacy). III. Mr. Peirce as a Critic (The *A Priori*; Determinism and Fatalism; Natural Laws, Descriptions; Causation; The Future in Mental Causation; Mental Causation). IV. Stray Shots. V. Retrospect.—*The Monist*, Vol. III., No. 4, page 571.

MONISM AND HENISM. A controversy with Lester F. Ward and Dr. Robert Lewins, criticising the materialistic and the solipsistic conceptions of monism.—*The Monist*, Vol. IV., No. 2, page 228. The same subject is treated in "Mind Not a Storage of Energy," in reply to Mr. Lester F. Ward.—*The Monist*, Vol. V., No. 2, page 282.

THE METAPHYSICAL x IN COGNITION. The Faust Attitude in Philosophy; Professor Jodl's Discrimination Between Scientific Knowledge and Philosophical Knowledge; Locke's Unknowable Essence of Things; Hume's Scepticism; Kant's Identification of the Ideal and the Subjective; Professor Deussen's Attempt at Modernising Metaphysics; Philosophy Defined; The Monistic Conception Outlined; Professor Mach's Anti-Mechanicalism in Physics; The Metaphysical x Not Unknown: The Conclusion,—*The Monist*, Vol. V., No. 4, page 510.

ON CHINESE PHILOSOPHY. Introductory; The Yang and the Yin; Fu Hi and Yu; The Yih and the Kwa; The Milfoil and the Spirit Tortoise; The Map of Ho and the Writing of Loh; The Great Plan in Nine Divisions; The T'ai Kih, the Ultimate Ground of Existence; The Monism of Chinese Philosophy, or Cheu-tsz's Philosophy; Chu Hi's Doctrine of Li and K'i the Immaterial Principle and Primary Matter; Filial Piety; The Significance of the Yih; T:en and Shang Ti, the Belief in a Personal God; Lao-tsz' and Confucius; Conclusion.—*The Monist*, Vol. VI., No. 2, page 188.

A DISCUSSION ON AGNOSTICISM, including a discussion of Professor Haeckel's monism.—*The Open Court*, Vol. V., No. 212.

THE IMPORTANCE OF CLEARNESS AND THE CHARM OF HAZINESS.—*The Open Court*, Vol. V., No. 209.

PSYCHOLOGY.

THE SOUL OF MAN. An Investigation of the Facts of Physiological and Experimental Psychology. Pages, 458. Illustrations, 152. Price, Cloth, $3.00.— I. The Philosophical Problem of Mind (Feeling and Motion; Is the Soul a Mechanism? The Origin of Mind). II. The Rise of Organised Life (Vitalism; Memory; Feeling as a Physiological Process). III. The Physiology of the Brain (the development of the brain from moner to man, profusely illustrated). IV. The Immortality of the Race and the Data of Propagation (the problems of fecundation and sex formation). V. Experimental Psychology (Hypnotism; Somnambulism; Dreams; Hallucinations; Suggestion; Dangers of Hypnotism). VI. The Ethical and Religious Aspects of Soul-Life (Pleasure; Pain; Nature of Thought; Rise of Consciousness; Whence Came Death? Immortality; The Soul of the Universe).

ARTICLES.

SOME QUESTIONS OF PSYCHO-PHYSICS. A controversy with Prof. Ernst Mach, a disquisition on the parallelism between feeling and motion, which arrives at the conclusion that feeling and motion are two abstractions of the same process. They are not identical but they are one. They are different and yet inseparable. As to the origin of life, the differences of soul and body are recognised. Ideas such as we read in books do not consist of paper and ink, nor do paper and ink contain ideas, nor can paper and ink be regarded as a physical basis of ideas, and yet ideas do not possess a ghost-like existence as things-in-themselves.—*The Monist*, Vol. I., No. 3, page 401.

OPTICAL PARADOXES. A review of Prof. Franz Brentano's article on the same subject.—*The Monist*, Vol. III., No. 4, page 651.

ON THE NATURE OF PLEASURE AND PAIN. In Comment on Professor Ribot's Theory.—*The Monist*, Vol. VI., No. 3, page 432.

ETHICS, RELIGION, ETC.

HOMILIES OF SCIENCE. Pages, 310. Cloth, Gilt Top, $1.50. —Fifty-nine brief sermons preached from the standpoint of science, on topics such as : Religion Based on Facts ; Religion of Progress ; Ethics of Evolution ; Design in Nature ; Conceptions of God ; The Conquest of Death ; Immortality and Science ; Free Thought, Its Truth and Its Error ; The Liberal's Folly; The Ethics of Struggle ; Monogamy; Aristocratomania ; Do We Want a Revolution ? The American Ideal ; etc.

THE RELIGION OF SCIENCE. Pages, 131. Price, Cloth, 50 cents; Paper, 25 cents.—A Systematic Exposition of the Doctrines of a Religion Based Upon the Facts of Both the Religious Life and the Investigations of Science. The booklet contains nine chapters: I. Doctrines Not Dogmas; II. The Authority for Conduct; III. Ethics; IV. The Nature of the Soul; V. The Importance of Immortality; VI. Mythology and Religion; VII. Christ and the Christians (including an inquisition on prayer); VIII. The Catholicity of Religion; and IX. Reply to a Freethinker.

THE ETHICAL PROBLEM. Three Lectures. I. Ethics, a Science; II. The Data of Ethics; III. Theories of Ethics. Pages, 105. Price, Cloth, 50 cents; Paper, 30 cents.—These Lectures are a criticism of the ethical movements which proclaim an ethics without reference to any authority for conduct, be it religious, scientific, or philosophical.

THE IDEA OF GOD. Fourth edition, revised and enlarged. Pages, 33. Paper, 15 cents.—I. The Nature of Ideas; II. The Etymology of the Word God; III. God an Abstract Idea; IV. The Conceptions of God; V. Definition of the Idea of God; VI. Entheism the Monistic Conception of God.

SCIENCE A RELIGIOUS REVELATION. An Address Delivered Before the World's Congress of Religions at Chicago, Ill.—Pages, 21. Paper, 5 cents.

ARTICLES.

THE CRITERION OF ETHICS AN OBJECTIVE REALITY. A controversy with Prof. Harald Höffding. The utilitarians consider the greatest amount of happiness of the greatest number as the criterion of Ethics, which is a subjective criterion. Scientific ethics, however, must be based upon an objective criterion. There is no objection to utilitarianism, but there is an objection to defining utility in terms of pleasure. As justice cannot be established by majority vote, so the greatest happiness of the greatest number is no criterion for that which is morally good.—*The Monist*, Vol. I., No. 4, page 552.

THE CLERGY'S DUTY OF ALLEGIANCE TO DOGMA AND THE STRUGGLE BETWEEN WORLD-CONCEPTIONS. The dawn of a new world-conception with a deeper scientific insight into the facts of experience, imperceptibly changes the significance of religious dogmas and the problem arises, Are clergymen under the obligation of believing the dogmas of the church in the old interpretation, or are they at liberty to change the interpretation of the dogmas in accordance with a more scientific conception? The reply is that their oath of allegiance is made in the bona fide conviction that the dogmas are the truth. The implications of this problem are discussed in detail from the legal standpoint, and parallel instances are quoted from other fields.—*The Monist*, Vol. II., No. 2, page 278.

LABOR DAY.—*The Open Court*, No. 367. A discussion of I. Labor as Drudgery; II. Origin and Nature of Labor; III. Blessings of Labor; IV. Dignity of Labor; V. The Labor Problem.

ETHICS AND THE COSMIC ORDER. A Criticism of Prof. Thomas H. Huxley's Position. Insists on ethics being in agreement with and derivable from the cosmic order of the universe.—*The Monist*, Vol. IV., No. 3, page 403.

THE LATE PROFESSOR ROMANES'S "THOUGHTS ON RELIGION."—*The Monist*, Vol. V., No. 3, page 385.

PROF. ADOLF HARNACK ON THE RELIGION OF SCIENCE.—*The Monist*, Vol. IV., No. 4, page 494.

THE MESSAGE OF MONISM TO THE WORLD.—*The Monist*, Vol. IV,, No. 4, page 545.

DEBATE ON CHRISTIAN MISSIONS.—*The Monist*, Vol. V., No. 2, page 274. The question whether or not a religious propaganda is right is answered in the affirmative, for that religion is dead whose adherents have no desire to propagate their faith.

THE WORLD'S RELIGIOUS PARLIAMENT EXTENSION. —*The Monist*, Vol. V., No. 3, page 345. The first annual report of the movement.

THE DAWN OF A NEW RELIGIOUS ERA —*The Monist*, Appendix to Vol. IV., No. 3, page 481. A review of the history of the Religious Parliament and its significance.

KARMA AND NIRVÂNA.—*The Monist*, Vol. IV., No. 3, page 417.

BUDDHISM AND CHRISTIANITY.—*The Monist*, Vol. V., No. 1, page 65.

THE NEW ORTHODOXY.—*The Monist*, Vol. VI., No. 1, page 91.

IS THE INFINITE A RELIGIOUS IDEA?—*The Open Court*, Vol. V., No. 185.

THE ANALYSIS OF THE MORAL OUGHT.—*The Open Court*, Vol. VI., No. 236.

REASON AND FAITH.—*The Open Court*, Vol. VI., No. 244.

IN A LIGHTER VEIN.

KARMA. A Story of Early Buddhism. A tale which was translated into French by Laurence Jerrold, editor of *Magazine International*; into German by Prof. Ludwig Büchner; and into Russian by Count Leo Tolstoï. Count Tolstoï writes about *Karma*: "I have read this tale to children and they liked it.

"And amongst grown-up people its reading always gave rise "to conversation about the gravest problems of life. And, to "my mind, that is a very good recommendation."—Printed in Japan on crêpe paper, and quaintly illustrated by Japanese artist. Price, 75 cents.

TRUTH IN FICTION, twelve tales with a moral, containing *The Chief's Daughter*, illustrating the ethics of sacrifice; *The Philosopher's Martyrdom*, a satire on agnosticism; *Capital and Labor*, a discussion of the difficulties of the labor problem pointing out its solution; *Ben Midrash*, the gardener of Galilee, a religio-psychical sketch.—Bound in white and gold. Gilt edges. Pages, 111. Price, $1.00.

THE OPEN COURT

A WEEKLY MAGAZINE

DEVOTED TO THE RELIGION OF SCIENCE

THE OPEN COURT does not understand by religion any creed or dogmatic belief, but man's world-conception in so far as it regulates his conduct.

The old dogmatic conception of religion is based upon the science of past ages; to base religion upon the maturest and truest thought of the present time is the object of *The Open Court*. Thus, the religion of *The Open Court* is the Religion of Science, that is, the religion of verified and verifiable truth.

Although opposed to irrational orthodoxy and narrow bigotry, *The Open Court* does not attack the properly religious element of the various religions. It criticises their errors unflinchingly but without animosity, and endeavors to preserve of them all that is true and good.

The current numbers of *The Open Court* contain valuable original articles from the pens of distinguished thinkers. Accurate and authorised translations are made in Philosophy, Science, and Criticism from the periodical literature of Continental Europe, and reviews of noteworthy recent investigations are presented.

Terms: $1.00 a year; $1.50 to foreign countries in the Postal Union. Single Copies, 5 cents.

THE MONIST

A QUARTERLY MAGAZINE OF

PHILOSOPHY AND SCIENCE.

THE MONIST discusses the fundamental problems of Philosophy in their practical relations to the religious, ethical, and sociological questions of the day. The following have contributed to its columns:

Prof. Joseph Le Conte, Prof. G. J. Romanes, Prof. C. Lombroso,
Dr. W. T. Harris, Prof. C. Lloyd Morgan, Prof. E. Haeckel,
M. D. Conway, James Sully, Prof. H. Höffding,
Charles S. Peirce, B. Bosanquet, Dr. F. Oswald,
Prof. F. Max Müller, Dr. A. Binet, Prof. J. Delbœuf,
Prof. E. D. Cope, Prof. Ernst Mach, Prof. F. Jodl,
Carus Sterne, Rabbi Emil Hirsch, Prof. H. M. Stanley,
Mrs. C. Ladd Franklin, Lester F. Ward. G. Ferrero,
Prof. Max Verworn, Prof. H. Schubert, J. Venn,
Prof. Felix Klein, Dr. Edm. Montgomery, Prof. H. von Holst.

Per Copy, 50 cents; Yearly, $2.00. In England and all countries in U.P.U. per Copy, 2s 6d; Yearly, 9s 6d.

CHICAGO:

THE OPEN COURT PUBLISHING CO.,

Monon Building, 324 Dearborn Street.

LONDON ADDRESS: 17 Johnson's Court, Fleet St., E. C.

CATALOGUE OF PUBLICATIONS

OF THE

OPEN COURT PUBLISHING CO.

MÜLLER, F. MAX.

THREE INTRODUCTORY LECTURES ON THE SCIENCE OF THOUGHT.
With a correspondence on "Thought Without Words," between F. Max Müller and Francis Galton, the Duke of Argyll, George J. Romanes and others. 128 pages. Cloth, 75 cents. Paper, 25 cents.

THREE LECTURES ON THE SCIENCE OF LANGUAGE.
The Oxford University Extension Lectures, with a Supplement, "My Predecessors," an essay on the genesis of "The Science of Thought." 112 pages. Second Edition. Cloth, 75 cents. Paper, 25 cents.

ROMANES, GEORGE JOHN.

DARWIN AND AFTER DARWIN.
An Exposition of the Darwinian Theory and a Discussion of Post Darwinian Questions. Two Vols., $3.00. Singly, as follows:

1. THE DARWINIAN THEORY. 460 pages. 125 illustrations. Cloth, $2.00.
2. POST-DARWINIAN QUESTIONS. Edited by Prof. C, Lloyd Morgan. Pages, 338. Cloth, $1.50.

AN EXAMINATION OF WEISMANNISM.
236 pages. Cloth, $1.00

THOUGHTS ON RELIGION.
Edited by Charles Gore, M. A., Canon of Westminster. Second Edition. Pages, 184. Cloth, gilt top, $1.25.

COPE, E. D.

THE PRIMARY FACTORS OF ORGANIC EVOLUTION.
121 cuts. *Circa* 550 pages. Cloth, $2.00.

RIBOT, TH.

THE PSYCHOLOGY OF ATTENTION.
Authorised translation, 121 pages. Cloth, 75 cents. Paper, 25 cents.

THE DISEASES OF PERSONALITY.
Authorised translation, 157 pages. Cloth, 75 cents. Paper, 25 cents.

THE DISEASES OF THE WILL.
Authorised translation, 134 pages. Cloth, 75 cents. Paper, 25 cents.
N. B. Full set, cloth, net, $1.75.

MACH, ERNST.

THE SCIENCE OF MECHANICS.
A CRITICAL AND HISTORICAL EXPOSITION OF ITS PRINCIPLES. Translated by T. J. MCCORMACK. 250 cuts. 518 pages. ½ m., gilt top. $2.50.

POPULAR SCIENTIFIC LECTURES.
313 pages. Cloth, gilt top. Net, $1.00.

THE ANALYSIS OF THE SENSATIONS.
(In preparation.)

FREYTAG, GUSTAV.

THE LOST MANUSCRIPT.
A Novel. Authorised translation. Two volumes. 953 pages. Extra cloth, gilt top, $4.00; in one volume, cloth, $1.00; paper, 75 cents.

GOODWIN, REV. T. A.

LOVERS THREE THOUSAND YEARS AGO.
As Indicated by the Song of Solomon. Enfield paper; gilt top. 42 pages. 50 cents.

CORNILL, CARL HEINRICH.

THE PROPHETS OF ISRAEL.
Popular Sketches from Old Testament History. Frontispiece, Michael Angelo's Moses. Pages, 210. Cloth, $1.00.

THE RISE OF THE PEOPLE OF ISRAEL.
See *Epitomes of Three Sciences*, below.

BINET, ALFRED.

THE PSYCHIC LIFE OF MICRO-ORGANISMS.
Authorised translation. 135 pages. Cloth, 75 cents; Paper, 25 cents.

ON DOUBLE CONSCIOUSNESS.
New Studies in Experimental Psychology. 93 pages. Paper, 15 cents.

TRUMBULL, M. M.

THE FREE TRADE STRUGGLE IN ENGLAND.
Second Edition. 296 pages. Cloth, 75 cents; paper, 25 cents.

WHEELBARROW: ARTICLES AND DISCUSSIONS ON THE LABOR QUESTION.
With portrait of the author. 303 pages. Cloth, $1.00; paper, 35 cents.

EARL GREY ON RECIPROCITY AND CIVIL SERVICE REFORM.
With Comments by Gen. M. M. Trumbull. Price, 10 cents.

GOETHE AND SCHILLER'S XENIONS.

Selected and Translated by Paul Carus. Printed in Album form; gilt edges. 162 pages. Cloth, $1.00.

CARUS, PAUL.

THE ETHICAL PROBLEM.
90 pages. Cloth, 50 cents; Paper, 30 cents.

FUNDAMENTAL PROBLEMS.
The Method of Philosophy as a Systematic Arrangement of Knowledge. Second edition, enlarged and revised. 372 pages. Cloth, $1.50.

HOMILIES OF SCIENCE.
310 pages. Cloth, Gilt Top, $1.50.

THE IDEA OF GOD.
32 pages. Paper, 15 cents.

THE SOUL OF MAN.
An Investigation of the Facts of Physiological and Experimental Psychology. With 152 cuts and diagrams. 458 pages. Cloth, $3.00.

TRUTH IN FICTION. TWELVE TALES WITH A MORAL.
Fine laid paper, white and gold binding, gilt edges. Pp. 128. $1.00.

THE RELIGION OF SCIENCE.
Extra edition. Price, 50 cents.

PRIMER OF PHILOSOPHY.
240 pages. Cloth, $1.00.

THE GOSPEL OF BUDDHA. According to Old Records.
Third Revised Edition. 275 pages. Cloth, Gilt Top, $1.00. Paper 35 cents.

KARMA. A STORY OF EARLY BUDDHISM.
Beautifully and quaintly illustrated by Japanese artists. Crêpe paper 75 cents.

GARBE, RICHARD.

THE REDEMPTION OF THE BRAHMAN. A TALE OF HINDU LIFE.
Laid paper. Veg. parch. binding. Gilt top. 96 pages. Price, 75 cents

EPITOMES OF THREE SCIENCES.

1. THE STUDY OF SANSKRIT. By *Prof. H. Oldenberg.*
2. EXPERIMENTAL PSYCHOLOGY. By *Prof. Joseph Jastrow.*
3. THE RISE OF THE PEOPLE OF ISRAEL. By *Prof. C. H. Cornill.*
140 pages. Cloth, 75 cents,

The Religion of Science Library.

A collection of bi-monthly publications, most of which are reprints of books published by The Open Court Publishing Company. Yearly, $1.50. Separate copies according to prices quoted. The books are printed upon good paper, from large type.

The Religion of Science Library, by its extraordinarily reasonable price, will bring a large number of valuable books within the reach of all readers.

The following have already appeared in the series:

No. 1. *The Religion of Science.* By PAUL CARUS. 25c.
2. *Three Introductory Lectures on the Science of Thought.* By F. MAX MÜLLER. 25c.
3. *Three Lectures on the Science of Language.* By F. MAX MÜLLER. 25c.
4. *The Diseases of Personality.* By TH. RIBOT. 25c.
5. *The Psychology of Attention.* By TH RIBOT. 25c.
6. *The Psychic Life of Micro-Organisms.* By ALFRED BINET. 25c.
7. *The Nature of the State.* By PAUL CARUS. 15c.
8. *On Double Consciousness.* By ALFRED BINET. 15c.
9. *Fundamental Problems.* By PAUL CARUS. 50c.
10. *The Diseases of the Will.* By TH. RIBOT. 25c.
11. *The Origin of Language.* By LUDWIG NOIRÉ. 15c.
12. *The Free Trade Struggle in England.* By M. M. TRUMBULL. 25c.
13. *Wheelbarrow on the Labor Question.* By M. M. TRUMBULL. 35c.
14. *The Gospel of Buddha.* By PAUL CARUS. 35c.
15. *The Primer of Philosophy.* By PAUL CARUS. 25c.
16. *On Memory,* and *The Specific Energies of the Nervous System.* By PROF. EWALD HERING. 15 cents.
17. *The Redemption of the Brahman.* A Tale of Hindu Life. By RICHARD GARBE. 25 cents.

The following are in preparation:

The Philosophy of Ancient India. By PROF. RICHARD GARBE.
Buddhism and Christianity. By PAUL CARUS.
The Lost Manuscript. A Novel. By GUSTAV FREYTAG.
The Study of Sanskrit. By PROF. H. OLDENBERG.
Old Testament History. By PROF. C. H. CORNILL.
On Germinal Selection. By PROF. AUGUST WEISMANN.

THE OPEN COURT PUBLISHING CO.,

324 DEARBORN STREET, CHICAGO, ILL.

LONDON ADDRESS: 17 Johnson's Court, Fleet St., E. C.